THE BEGINNINGS OF THE CHURCH
IN THE NEW TESTAMENT

The Beginnings of the Church
in the New Testament

Essays by
FERDINAND HAHN
AUGUST STROBEL
EDUARD SCHWEIZER

Translated by
IAIN and UTE NICOL

AUGSBURG PUBLISHING HOUSE
MINNEAPOLIS, MINNESOTA

This book was originally published in German under the title, *Die Anfänge der Kirche im Neuen Testament*, copyright © 1967 by Vandenhoeck and Ruprecht in Göttingen.

Translation copyright © THE SAINT ANDREW PRESS, 1970

Biblical quotations are from the
Revised Standard Version

Library of Congress Catalog Card No. 79-121046

First published in the United States of America, 1970

Printed in Great Britain

CONTENTS

PREFACE

THE repeated attempt to research into the beginnings of the Christian faith and to make a critical comparison of these beginnings with its present situation is one of the principles of reformation thought. For generations Evangelical Theology has occupied itself with the question of the historical Jesus as a basic datum of the Christian faith. Simple as this question appeared to be, it was, and still is a difficult one to answer. Due to the intermingling of history with the special situation of the witnesses in the texts, and with the expectations of those who interpret and listen to the texts today, innumerable questions have arisen in addition to this first and basic one. One of these questions, and certainly one of the most interesting, is the question of the historical beginnings of what we call the church. Did Jesus himself 'found' a church? If not, where are we to look for the beginnings of the 'church'? One primary clue is the fact of a group of disciples which Jesus gathered around himself. What can we know about the historicity of this group of disciples and about the real nature of Jesus' call to discipleship? How did the pre-Easter group of disciples become the post-Easter Christian community? How did those who awaited the end of the world become a community which developed its own forms, found a place for itself in the world and yet at the same time remained distinct from the world? These are questions which throw a critical light upon our own Christianity and our own understanding of the church. The essays presented in this book are an attempt to provide some answers to these questions with the help of up-to-date theological research. They are based on papers given to a theological study-group organised by the Evangelical Academy in Tutzing in March 1966. We should like to express our thanks to the speakers and authors for their work and for the effort they have put into it.

Tutzing, Summer 1967   PAUL RIEGER.

Pre-Easter Discipleship

By FERDINAND HAHN

FOR modern man historical questioning and research are not only accepted facts, they have become absolutely necessary in so far as he struggles for an intelligible clarification of his own place in history and as he faces the tasks which are set before him in a responsible way. If we want to understand our present, our own existence, and the way towards the future, we simply cannot avoid questioning the past and all that has emerged from the past.

But even where the biblical witness and Christian faith are concerned, historical questioning and investigation leave us somewhat dissatisfied. The different branches of historical criticism have made it possible for us to find new approaches and have opened up new fields which provide us with new insight into the texts of the Old and New Testaments. We are learning more and more to understand the biblical writings from the point of view of their own presuppositions and, most of all, to differentiate between original reports and the later interpretations, which in the long tradition of the church have been superimposed upon the original meanings and which have tended to obscure them. To a large extent we can also make distinctions within the biblical tradition. In the New Testament we are concerned in this context not only with the numerous layers of tradition within primitive Christianity which belong to different periods and regions. The question which is also forced upon us, is that of the historical Jesus, his activity and proclamation on the one hand, and on the other, the post-Easter message of the early church. In the Gospels, history and proclamation are closely interwoven; pre-Easter history is seen in the light of the cross and resurrection, and the faith to which in the meantime the disciples have come, colours the presentation of Jesus' earthly ministry. Nevertheless we have to try to separate these different elements in order to define the

9

historical Jesus more closely. For this task, theological exegesis can provide us with the necessary tools.

The premises underlying the historical-critical interpretation of the Bible constantly expose themselves to re-examination, but, where faith is at stake, it is to the reality of history which the biblical witness itself points and in a way quite unprecedented in the ancient world. According to the witness of the Bible, the fact that God acts in history, that in a definite historical event He has brought about a new era, that—in the words of John 1 : 14—'the Word became flesh', all this gives us justification for posing questions about history and at the same time permits us to apply the appropriate historical methods.[1]

It is generally agreed that the fulness of the biblical message cannot be entirely comprehended in a purely historical way. Nevertheless, we should not underestimate the fact that it is precisely by means of historical investigation that, circumstances permitting, we are brought very close to the facts of the matter. This is especially evident where the proclamation and activity of Jesus are concerned. We shall therefore begin with the pre-Easter history of Jesus, then we shall go on to deal with the question of Easter itself, then finally with the post-Easter period.

I

In the New Testament, to follow and to be a disciple are two concepts which stand in a mutual relationship with one another: he who follows Jesus is his disciple, and whoever wishes to be his disciple must be prepared to follow him.

But what does it mean to follow? What does it mean especially with regard to the earthly ministry of Jesus? We shall begin with those texts which make this aspect particularly clear and which will help us to find a proper answer.

Mark 2 :14 gives us a concise but very instructive account of the call of Levi, the tax collector. At first sight this story looks like an incidental insertion which serves as an introduction to the following account of Jesus' table-fellowship with the tax collectors (verses 15-17). The fact is however, that this is an independent text and it is of special importance for us because the report of the incident is so compressed that the basic features of the incident stand out with special clarity.

The text runs as follows: 'And as he passed on, he (Jesus) saw Levi the son of Alphaeus sitting at the tax office, and he said to him, "Follow me," and he rose and followed him'.

This story of the call of Levi has three parts which are clearly distinguishable. First of all Jesus' encounter with the tax collector is briefly depicted, then as the main part of the account there follows the call, then finally we are told how this man obeys the summons of Jesus.

Let us now clarify this in more detail. First of all there are some important observations to be made about the brevity of the description of this encounter. It is said here of Jesus that he saw this man 'as he passed on' and then called him. If we read only this one story there is nothing in particular which arouses our attention. If, however, we also take into consideration the fact that exactly the same is said in the accounts which deal with the call of Simon and Andrew, we may assume that this is something very significant and has therefore been carefully preserved in the reports. That Jesus called men to discipleship as he passed by is therefore not simply mere historical reminiscence. The emphasis is rather upon the fact of the peculiarly unconditional nature of the call. What is decisive here is not an exact knowledge of the person, nor their gradually developed familiarity with one another, but a quite astonishing immediacy.

This observation is strengthened when we take into account the information which is given about Levi. His name is given exactly: 'Levi the son of Alphaeus'.[2] Despite the brevity of the report neither does the rest of the story lack in graphic detail: Levi is sitting in front of the tax office, at his place of work and carrying out his duties. But what sort of profession is this? The Romans had introduced a very stiff system of taxation, but had arranged things in such a way as to make it comparatively easy for themselves. They had transferred the right to raise taxes to a number of publicans who were obliged to yield to them very large sums of money, but who had complete freedom to choose their own methods of exacting payment and also to devise means of lining their own pockets. In their turn the publicans had appointed tax collectors whom they treated

11

in the same way; Levi is such a tax collector. We can easily imagine that with this kind of arrangement greed and dishonesty, despotism and cruelty, were rife among the publicans and among the tax collectors as well. It was for this reason that tax collectors were generally outlawed, by the pious on the one hand because they flouted the Jewish law, and by the rest of the people as well because of their collaboration with the occupying forces.

Such a short introduction made the situation immediately clear to Jesus' hearers. Therefore the words 'Follow me', which form the centre of our story are all the more surprising. Jesus issues his call to men as he passes by, and even tax collectors are included! What matters here are neither the positive nor negative assumptions of the persons concerned; the important thing is that in this encounter, which seen from outside might appear quite accidental, a decision is made.

Jesus did not allow any conditions to come between himself and others. This is clearly illustrated in his attitude towards the tax collectors. He was not afraid to enter their homes and share their meals, although for the Jews this was taboo. Not without reason was he called 'a friend of tax collectors and sinners'[3] and it was because of his readiness to cross the barriers of fixed social customs that he caused a great deal of offence and made many enemies.

We must take note of another characteristic feature of the call to discipleship: no reasons or explanations are given, there is no why or wherefore. There is simply this one Word, a call which at the same time is a demand and which comes with an astonishing immediacy. And just as Jesus' call is totally unconditional, so the response must also be unconditional. And in response to the call which comes with authoritative power what is required is unqualified obedience.

Then at the end of the story it simply says: 'and he rose and followed him'. This man is prepared to obey without hesitation and without further inquiry. He entrusts his life and his destiny to the one who has called him to discipleship. With this encounter and this decision something entirely new begins, therefore he leaves his job and sets out to share his life with Jesus and his followers.

According to Mark 1 : 16-20 exactly the same happens when

Jesus calls the brothers Simon and Andrew and James and John. Mark I : 15-18 tell us that as he was 'passing along'[4] he saw Simon and Andrew the brother of Simon casting a net in the sea; for they were fishermen. And Jesus said to them, "Follow me and I will make you become fishers of men". And immediately they left their nets and followed him'.

So much for the account of the first call. Here again the emphasis is placed upon the fact that Jesus was passing by and that the men were to be found doing their everyday work; then there comes the Word of Jesus' call, given here in the ancient Semitic form of expression: 'Follow me', (or more literally: 'come, come after me'); then finally the report of the outcome: 'And immediately they left their nets and followed him'.

The only thing which distinguishes this text from Mark 2 : 14 is that the call is given in two parts: 'Follow me—and I will make you become fishers of men'. Therefore the beginning of the story does not merely describe how the brothers were casting their nets, but stresses: 'for they were fishermen'. A new occupation will take the place of their old one, and this is made quite clear by means of a pictorial expression which for that time was downright offensive: 'I will make you become fishers of men'. This way of speaking could easily cause offence. But quite often Jesus did not hesitate to use words which were unusual and which might even scandalise his hearers.[5]

The call to Levi is a call which is primarily unconditional. But Mark 1 : 16-18 stresses that discipleship is a call to service and that this demands every effort from the person concerned for a special task. We shall return to this aspect later.

Mark 1 : 16-18 and Mark 2 : 14 have the character of independent, well-balanced stories. Mark 1 : 19f., from the point of view of its form, is an appendix: 'And going on a little farther, he saw James the son of Zebedee and John his brother, who were in their boat mending the nets. And immediately he called them; and they left their father Zebedee in the boat with the hired servants, and followed him.' The beginning of the story again gives a brief description of the men doing their work, and at the end we are told how both men leave their father Zebedee and the hired servants behind.

But the actual Word of Jesus' call is not repeated; rather, it says: 'And immediately he called them'. Now the theological concept of the call takes the place of Jesus' actual call to discipleship. This is because the stories are parallel and because it also avoids literal repetition. However, we can recognise here an advanced stage of theological reflection.

Reviewing these three calls to discipleship, which with the help of the text we have examined in some detail, we are now in a position to ask: does the way in which the text reports these events reflect what actually took place? There can be no doubt that we are dealing with a fairly fixed form of story. The early church formed and shaped such units of the tradition with great care. For decades they were handed down orally and therefore they had to be carefully preserved in case they should lose their central meaning through careless repetition. The second stage came when they were woven into the wider context of a gospel. There is no doubt that a certain amount of stereotyping came into them as well. What happened to these men in their encounter with Jesus is a criterion of the idea of discipleship as such. Obviously, the reports are also theologically very concentrated. Special attention is given to the main features and all irrelevant details can be omitted. However, the immediacy of the call to discipleship and the unconditional nature of the demand for obedience are not later additions to the text. Therefore we should not attempt to give a greater reality to the stories by bringing in unnecessary historical and psychological considerations. Their once-for-all nature is so obvious that we must regard them in each instance as pre-Easter events. We have to admit that there are limits to our historical knowledge and these limits have to be respected. This is also the case with regard to those whom Jesus called as well as for his own ministry and conduct. At all events we must begin with the assumption that these texts simply take the efficacy of Jesus' call as something for granted and assume also that this call could be accepted in its immediacy.

II

If we are to put the idea of discipleship into its proper context and to understand its own particular characteristics[6] we must now go on to look briefly at its background in the Old Testament and in contemporary Judaism.

There is no parallel to this idea in the *Greek tradition* nor in the Hellenistic milieu. Of course there is the concept of *akolouthein*, which was taken up by the later church and transformed so as to correspond with its own particular assumptions. However, this word means 'following' in the sense of imitation. But the idea of *imitatio* is quite alien to the original early Christian tradition. It is taken up only now and then by the later Hellenistic communities but is of no decisive importance for the New Testament as a whole.[7] During certain periods in the course of the history of the church the idea of the *Imitatio Christi* gained considerable importance. However, it is not necessary to discuss this question here.[8] There is then a distinct difference between the Greek idea of discipleship and the New Testament idea. The Greek talks about discipleship as the imitation of God, whereas, in almost every case, the New Testament speaks about discipleship as a relationship to Jesus.[9]

If we examine the Old Testament and Jewish background we shall discover that this is not accidental. Followers of Jesus can be compared with those who followed the prophets and the scribes, and the idea of discipleship stands in line with those notions of discipleship which were prevalent in the prophetic schools and also among the companies of pupils which every rabbi gathered around himself. This is also the context from which the New Testament idea of following is derived, and which in a purely literal sense means 'to come after someone', as we already saw in Mark 1 : 17.

During the inter-testamental period doctrine became very important. This consisted in instruction in the Law or Torah.[10] The people had to be instructed in the Holy Scriptures, especially in the Pentateuch. This was done mainly in the synagogues. For this purpose teachers and instructors had to be trained. They were selected from the groups of disciples who gathered around any acknowledged scribe and who were his 'followers'. The main task of the disciples was, in the strict sense of the word, to serve their masters. In addition to this, their masters would teach them the Torah and its proper interpretation. However, mere listening and learning was not

15

enough. It was also important that, day by day, in close association with their teachers, they should gain experience in the practical application of the Torah and so become accustomed to practising the Law themselves. Anyone who mastered the Law and the practice of the Law could then himself become a rabbi and leave the school of his master.[11]

This teacher-pupil relationship within Judaism is the continuation in a different form of the prophet-disciple relationship in the Old Testament. 'Following' has secular roots and basically means subordination and readiness to serve. It is used, for instance, with reference to the retinue of a king, or to the place of the bride or the wife in relation to her husband. Just as the images of marriage and adultery can be used to describe Israel's relationship to her God,[12] correspondingly, the Old Testament speaks about 'going after the Baals', or idols, and occasionally we find references to 'following Jahweh', the God of Israel.[13] But these metaphors are not particularly relevant to our problem. What is of importance for us is the idea of 'following' the prophets. Here, just as with the retinue of a king or with the bride and the wife, the main thing is a sharing of life in which subordination and duty are of decisive importance. Unfortunately, the Old Testament does not provide very much information about this. The fact that there were disciples of prophets cannot be denied. Regrettably however, we know very little about their position, their duties and their way of life together.[14] It is especially difficult to ascertain whether the disciples of the prophets themselves were given any definite prophetic task. Even though there was a number of official prophets,[15] it is unlikely that this was the rule. We simply cannot be certain on this point. Nevertheless, one figure is presented to us with some clarity and that is Elisha, the disciple of Elijah. We can say for certain that in his relationship to the prophet, service was of the first importance. In addition to this we can assume that they shared their lives very closely. Moreover, it is also quite clear that Elisha was destined not just to be a servant. The intention is that he should also assume the office of Elijah.

The account of Elijah's call is surprisingly similar to those stories in the New Testament which deal with the call to discipleship. Judging by their formal structure we can assume

16

that they are intentionally dependent upon this Old Testament text. A careful reading and comparison will make this quite clear. The passage we are concerned with is, 1 Kings 19 : 19-21:

(a) 'So he (Elijah) departed from there and found Elisha the son of Shaphat, who was ploughing, with twelve yoke of oxen before him, and he was with the twelfth.

(b) 'Elijah passed by him and cast his mantle upon him.

(c) 'And he left the oxen, and ran after Elijah, and said, "Let me kiss my father and my mother, and then I will follow you." And he said to him, "Go back again; for what have I done to you?" And he returned from following him, and took the yoke of oxen, and slew them, and boiled their flesh with the yokes of the oxen, and gave it to the people and they ate.

(d) 'Then he arose and went after Elijah, and ministered to him.'[16]

There is one obvious difference here from the scribal idea of discipleship. In the case which we have here, the pupil did not himself choose his master, rather it was Elijah who took the initiative. Later Jesus was to do the same when he called his disciples. Moreover, in the case of Elijah, discipleship comes as the result not of a spoken call, but of a prophetic sign.

Another striking feature of the story is that it is in four parts. As in the Gospel stories, the encounter is described first of all. Then there follows that act of calling with the casting of the mantle. The actual outcome does not follow immediately but only after the comparatively detailed farewell-scene.

It is quite clear that the New Testament stories are dependent upon this narrative form. Yet at the same time they differ. The most crucial difference is the omission of the third section, namely, the farewell-scene. The explanation for this is quite simple. In early Christianity the three-part form replaced the four-part because of a saying of Jesus which is recorded in Luke 9 : 61f.: 'Another said, "I will follow you, Lord; but let me first say farewell to those at my home." Jesus said to him, "No one who puts his hand to the plough and looks back is fit for the kingdom of God." '

Thus when it is a matter of following Jesus even the farewell from one's family has to be omitted. And according to a very similar saying of Jesus, the man who is called to discipleship may not even bury his own father. And to such a man Jesus says: 'Leave the dead to bury their own dead; but as for you, go and proclaim the kingdom of God' (Luke 9 : 59f.).

The change which takes place in the narratives dealing with discipleship in early Christianity is obviously quite intentional. This was inherently necessary. The discipleship of Jesus is certainly characterised by Old Testament and Jewish pre-suppositions, but it cannot be described entirely in terms of the framework of the Old Testament model. As we shall also see later, it is also not enough to say that Jesus' discipleship represents an intensification or radicalising when compared with the older forms of discipleship. Rather we have to say that discipleship acquires a quite different structure.

III

We shall now go on to elucidate further the special nature of Jesus' discipleship by examining some of its particular characteristics in more detail. We shall begin by taking up what we have already established about the difference between the Old Testament and New Testament narrative forms which deal with this theme.

What is it that is significant about a refusal to bid one's *family* farewell? The person who does bid his family farewell takes leave of them on good terms. On the other hand, when he simply goes away without saying goodbye he breaks off relations with them. This is also the case with the passage about burying one's father. This was a duty incumbent upon the son, and to leave the burial to others would not only be an offence against custom and devotion to one's family, it would also have been to violate the law of the time. In turn, such a person would therefore be regarded as an outcast by his closest relatives. How then can Jesus make such a demand? Among the Jews it was agreed that it was precisely this duty to one's family demanded by the Law which should not under any circumstances be surrendered or infringed. But it is no mere accident that among the words of Jesus we find a saying which for us is almost incredible: 'If any one comes to me and does not hate his own father and mother and wife and children and

18

brothers and sisters, yes, and even his own life, he cannot be my disciple', (Luke 14 : 26). 'Hate' of course does not denote the blind, objectionable passion which we mean when we use the word. Here it means to remain firmly at a distance. The disciple must consciously and resolutely distance himself from his closest relatives, in the same way as, and in the terms of the Old Testament, the God-fearing man must 'hate' every sin. In this context the point of the following saying of Jesus becomes intelligible: 'Do not think that I have come to bring peace on earth; I have not come to bring peace, but a sword,' (Matt. 10 : 34).

When we recall the stories about discipleship which we discussed at the beginning we meet with a further similar point. For Levi, as well as for the two pairs of brothers, discipleship involves giving up their *occupations*. We can well imagine that the disciple of a scribe would hardly be in a position to continue with his occupation and at the same time fulfil his task as a disciple. However this was not the case. It was necessary for the Jewish rabbi and his pupils to earn their own living and for this reason they had to learn and practise a trade.[17] It was by no means impossible to have a trade and to teach at the same time. In contrast to this, however, to follow Jesus means giving up one's daily occupation and taking up a new one in the service of Jesus. A disciple of Jesus has a task to fulfil which demands his whole life.[18] His livelihood is to be the concern of those he serves. The instruction that 'the labourer deserves his wages',[19] (Luke 10 : 7), is to be understood in that context. For the Christian community this became the accepted principle, even though Paul in most cases renounced this apostolic right and reverted to the Jewish practice because of the difficulties and problems which might otherwise have arisen for the preaching of the Gospel.[20] What is decisive is that he who is called to discipleship by Jesus must surrender himself completely and to such an extent that there can be no room left for any other regular occupation. Thus again it may be asked: How can Jesus make such a demand?

What is true of the family and of one's occupation is also true as regards *possessions*. The familiar story of the Rich Young Man (Mark 10 : 17ff., par. Matt. 19 : 16ff.), is really a

19

story about discipleship.[21] This is a fact which is often over-looked. One interpreter has described it as a story of Jesus' unsuccessful choice of a disciple.[22] This is certainly true, because every call to discipleship requires that the person must himself be prepared to obey. However, it is this readiness to obey which the Rich Young Man lacks. But the main emphasis in this story lies elsewhere. On the one hand, the point is made that the call of Jesus goes out to the righteous and the un-righteous alike, on the other hand it deals with this man's attitude to his possessions. For our present purpose we may leave aside the Rich Man's opening question about eternal life and the allusion to the Old Testament commandments. What must be taken into consideration is the fact that no matter how faithfully a person may keep the commandments, he is still far from having made the decision to follow and to be a disciple of Jesus. Here a claim arises which the Old Testament law, with all its variety, has not even envisaged. As far as the attitude to riches is concerned this man is confronted with an unequivocal Either-Or. Unlike some of the other stories about discipleship the Rich Man is told to go back home, but in this instance it is not to bid farewell to his relatives in the proper way, but in order to sell all his possessions and so burn his boats com-pletely. What is required of him also is a radical surrender of his whole past. He is expected as it were to bar his own way back by giving up all his possessions and distributing the proceeds to the poor.

But this is not only something which concerns a person's family, his occupation and his possessions. We have already come across the saying in Luke 14 : 26: 'If any one comes to me and does not hate his own father and mother . . . yes, and even his *own life*, he cannot be my disciple'. A person who is called upon to surrender everything that belongs to him could quite easily interpret such a demand in a legalistic way. But in fact, what is involved here is that a person surrender himself and thus bind himself completely to Jesus and his destiny. To give oneself in this way is simply an expression and also the ultimate consequence of the fact that he no longer belongs to himself but to another. This is related to the promise of eternal life which is expressed in Mark 10 : 29f., and which also refers to this surrender of family and possessions:

'Truly, I say to you, there is no one who has left house or brothers or sisters or mother or father or children or lands, for my sake . . . who will not receive . . . eternal life'.[23] And closely connected with this is the saying of warning and promise: 'Whoever would save his life will lose it; and whoever loses his life for my sake . . . will save it'.[24] This saying is directly connected with Mark 8 : 36f.: 'For what does it profit a man, to gain the whole world and forfeit his life?'[25] The setting for these two Logia is the well-known saying about taking up the cross (v. 34) which heads this group of sayings. The present form of this saying has most likely been influenced by the post-Easter community and was probably later formulated in the light of the events of the Passion. This therefore sums up the demand to take up one's cross and follow in view of the suffering and death of Jesus.[26] What at all events is essential to Jesus' own preaching and demand is that the disciple must go the way of his master, and that he will not be spared humiliation and suffering.

Discipleship therefore means to be totally bound to Jesus' person and his mission. It is precisely this which distinguishes it from any previous idea of discipleship. No prophet or scribe could demand or expect that a person should bind himself to his person in this way. The disciples of prophets and scribes eventually succeeded their masters. Discipleship was a preparatory stage and did not have the same determining effect upon a person as it had in the case of Jesus. Because of the exclusive nature of this bond, Jesus' single demand to follow him is now intelligible and is thus distinguished from every legalistic or casuistic definition of discipleship. This also throws light on the saying in Matt. 23 : 8: 'But you are not to be called rabbi, for you have one teacher, and you are all brethren'. To be a disciple of Jesus is a lasting bond. The disciple can never take the master's place no matter how much he works and preaches in order to fulfil his master's commission.

IV

It has not yet been made clear how Jesus can make such a radical demand, nor how he could expect his disciples to bind themselves to him without reservation. It would be a mistake to attempt to explain this with the help of the titles which were given to Jesus by the early church. Such titles as Christ, Lord, Son of Man and Son of God certainly aim at explaining what Jesus' life and ministry meant. However, in any attempt to present Jesus' pre-Easter activity we have to go behind the christological preaching of the disciples.[27]

Jesus' own person occupies a position of unique importance. This can be seen particularly with regard to the call to discipleship. However, it is not his person which forms the centre of his own proclamation but rather his mission. His task is to proclaim *the advent of the kingdom of God*, and in his own activity the time of salvation comes in the midst of the old Aeon. The keynote of his proclamation is: 'The time is fulfilled, and the kingdom of God is at hand; repent, and believe in the gospel', (Mark 1 : 15).[28]

Jesus proclaims the good news of God's ultimate and gracious act of salvation towards men. Now men may already experience the advent and the ultimacy of the things to come in the midst of a lost and transitory world. The reign of God is present not only in the Word, but in the whole of Jesus' activity in which the advent of God's saving reign is taking place. This is true not only of the healings, the pronouncement of the forgiveness of sins, and the breaking down of the barriers erected against the outcasts, the 'tax collectors and sinners', but also of those instances where Jesus violates the sacred ordinances of the Old Testament, for example, in his attitude to the use of the Sabbath, his criticism of the law of Moses and in the cleansing of the temple by which he announces the end of cultic sacrifice as practised in Jerusalem.

This advent of the reign of God is to be understood as the inbreaking of the future upon the present. Therefore everything that happens in the present is not only related to the end but, what is more important, is conceivable only in terms of the end. In this sense it is a proleptic eschatological event. It can certainly be experienced. It cannot, however, be calculated in any inner-wordly fashion nor as being at man's disposal. It remains a contingent occurrence. It is not simply that something new happens which is then subsequently drawn into the

22

already existing inner-wordly structure. The eschatologically new is rather that which in every sense surpasses all that has gone before, for as God's final act it is qualitatively different. Therefore it is also not to be thought of as a new period, or as though the old historical epoch were now followed by a new one. Wherever the new happens, it happens in the form of the future reaching out into the present and running counter to our time and to our world.

Among the texts which express this best are the two figurative sayings in Mark 2 : 21f.: 'No one sews a piece of unshrunk cloth on an old garment; if he does, the patch tears away from it, the new from the old, and a worse tear is made. And no one puts new wine into old wineskins; if he does, the wine will burst the skins and the wine is lost, and so are the skins'. Thus any question about the continuity between the old and the new is authoritatively put aside. The intention of Jesus' Word is precisely to point out that the new does not merely make up for the deficiencies of the old or of that which already exists, nor is the new merely an improvement or a continuation of the old, but is directly opposed to it. The importance of this should not be overlooked or under-estimated in order to explain it in terms of a salvation-history which is continuous with the Old Testament covenantal history and its tradition. There can be no doubt that the coming of the eschatological reign of God is already contained within the horizon of God's already existing history with his people. This is especially true with regard to the Old Testament promises. But it is not God's actions in the past nor the promises which explain the eschatological event of salvation. Rather it is by looking back from this salvation-event that the promises are seen in a completely new light, and it is from the point of view of the fulfilment, which exceeds all the promises, that God's actions in history up to this point are to be understood.[29] Therefore the fact that the new runs counter to the old is something which must not be overlooked. The eschatological event is not, as the Old Testament and Judaism often expected it to be, a continuation of everything that has gone before nor a restoration of all that already exists to its original state. Even the idea of the restoration of the creation is insufficient as an explanation of the eschatological event. In the eschatological action of God everything that has gone before is brought to an end and replaced by a new and lasting reality.

With the coming of the eschatological reality every tie with the old must be broken. This explains the astonishing immediacy and the total claim which we find in those texts which were dealt with at the beginning. We have come to the conclusion that in comparison with the Old Testament and contemporary Jewish forms, the structure of discipleship has been profoundly changed and that its content has to be defined anew. It is now clear why this should be the case. With Jesus' message and action the new has come and the eschatological salvation now given by God has begun. This gives rise to the saying: 'Blessed are the eyes which see what you see! For I tell you that many prophets and kings desired to see what you see, and did not see it, and to hear what you hear, and did not hear it', (Luke 10 : 23f.).

It is for the sake of that which is new that Jesus calls men to discipleship. The call is a demand and a claim upon the whole man. There can be no 'not only—but also'. It is simply an Either-Or. The demands of Jesus as they are expressed in the sayings and stories about discipleship must be seen from this angle. To suggest that these are an intensification or radicalisation of the Old Testament commandments would be to say that they simply augment that which is already given. This is certainly not what is meant. It is quite true that according to Jesus' sayings the will of God may be discerned in the Old Testament commandments, but in the call to discipleship what really matters is something quite different from the commandments and the Law. The decisive thing about this discipleship is not a matter of obeying various instructions but of being totally bound to a person. In the different stories about discipleship Jesus makes certain specific demands, but these should by no means be understood as law, nor should they be reduced to the level of works. The radical nature of Jesus' demand is something which cannot be denied, but its ground is elsewhere. It springs from the newness of that which is to come and from the eschatological event which is already breaking in.

It is precisely because discipleship requires obedience to Jesus' authoritative Word, and not an action which might be defined in a legalistic sense, that certain warnings are issued to those who intend to become disciples. Whenever anyone came to Jesus and asked to be accepted as a disciple, as though he were a Jewish teacher, it was pointed out to him that something else was at stake. The parable of the Tower and the King going to War is to be read in the light of this fact, (Luke 14 : 28ff.). It closes with the words: 'So therefore, whoever of you does not renounce all that he has cannot be my disciple', (v. 33).[30] A similar answer is given to a man who says to Jesus: 'I will follow you wherever you go'. And Jesus said to him: 'Foxes have holes and birds of the air have nests; but the Son of Man has nowhere to lay his head', (Luke 9 : 57f.). Jesus' homelessness is the sign of his lowliness and of his way of suffering. It is on this way that a disciple has to be prepared to accompany him.

V

It is not difficult to understand that the question keeps cropping up as to how Jesus' demands concerning discipleship are to be fulfilled. The question also frequently arises whether Jesus did not simply allow people to remain in their own situations. There are in fact some hints of this in the New Testament. However, we should not make the mistake of classifying those to whom Jesus' call goes out as exceptional cases. If we were to do this we would also have to ask who was a disciple of Jesus in the true sense and who was not, why Jesus chose some to be disciples and not others. This would really not take us very far. One often also starts off from a false presupposition. Most people, when they hear the word 'disciples' think only of the 'Twelve'. But to equate the 'disciples' with the 'Twelve' is something which comes only at a later stage in the tradition and cannot therefore be original. In Matthew's Gospel this is taken for granted, but the older Gospel of Mark and the Lukan accounts show that the 'disciples' consisted of a larger circle and are therefore to be distinguished from the 'Twelve'.[31] We shall make reference to the 'Twelve' at a later stage. The circle of disciples was basically open and by no means exclusive. When we take this into account then we can see that discipleship is not to be

25

understood as confined to exceptional cases. The early church quite deliberately handed down the stories about discipleship as so-called paradigms,[32] and with the intention that they should serve as examples for every Christian. It would be a mistake to oversimplify this problem. It is rather the basic meaning of Jesus' demand which has to be taken seriously, for it is because of the radical nature of this demand that through the ages it has never ceased to leave people alone and which has kept them in a state of healthy unease.

It is very difficult to give a detailed description of what discipleship meant to different people at that time, or the form which this life-relationship to Jesus actually took. It is quite true that the Gospels do give more information about discipleship but this refers mainly to a few disciples who in most cases belong to the circle of the Twelve. Nevertheless, there is one essential feature of discipleship expressed in the story of the Rich Young Man, namely, that Jesus confronted men with a decision which called for a profound change in their lives and which meant that to follow him was to give up all that belonged to the past and to one's former way of life. What happened in individual cases cannot be generalised. This means that what discipleship is cannot be defined by merely adding up the different demands which meet us in these stories. It is rather the case that each one of these demands goes right to the heart of one's existence in a way which points out that what is required is one's whole life. The call to discipleship as it is issued to different people has an impact and intensity which can be compared with the authoritative Word by which Jesus cast out the demons. This call does not relieve a man of his freedom. Nevertheless, it confronts him with the inescapable question of whether he will obey or not. The coming of the reign of God becomes a reality for him in a single event, and when this takes place there can be no escape, nor is there any room for questions. Therefore the call to discipleship is *not* a call which goes out to exceptional cases, but to people in their own individual situations.

A man has to expose himself to this fundamental demand which claims each individual in his whole existence. And this is the case even if we are still confronted with the unsolved question of how this being totally bound to Jesus is to be

26

actually realised in the world in which we live. It is a demand which should not be modified, for it is a demand which claims the whole man for the eschatological reign of God. There can also be no question that the demand of Jesus does not merely touch the periphery of the realities of our world, it reaches right into the midst of them. This is why it is necessary to recognise and to take seriously this demand which has the power to act counter to the world in its established structures. We should certainly not imagine Jesus as an enthusiastic radical. On the other hand, the greater danger for us is to expect that he should always adjust himself to the existing order. Jesus never simply accepted existing structures without question. To put it in Bonhoeffer's terms, he is aware of the reality of the penultimate, but this penultimate is inescapably exposed to the critical light of the ultimate.[33]

The sayings of the Sermon on the Mount will help to illustrate this. These sayings are not just instances of a more consistent application of the commandment to love nor simply a means to a deeper understanding of the Old Testament commandments. What the commandment to love actually does is to abolish the individual commandments and along with them the question about what is permitted and what is not. The commandment to love calls also for total obedience, for it means to be totally bound to the will of God. However, total obedience can never be achieved or realised by means of legal prescriptions. On the other hand this does not mean that in the preaching of Jesus there are no longer any ethical directives at all. But just as is the case with the call to discipleship, the question also arises here as to whether and how it is possible to fulfil them.[34] With the recognition that it is impossible to systematise Jesus' demands much is gained. They cannot be connected together by placing them together and then trying to provide the missing links. Every single one of these demands expresses God's total and absolute will and it is as such that his will strikes home to man's heart. This is what we find demonstrated in the demands of Jesus. They are in no sense aimed at the vast area of forms of human conduct in the world but at placing man under the claim of the ultimate. Of course this also has an effect in the sphere of the penultimate. But this is not to say that a systematic framework is provided for it.

And it is for this reason also that there is no such thing as a hierarchic system of discipleship in the proclamation of Jesus.[35]

The demands of Jesus break into the existing transitory world with an extraordinary power. This is because they are formulated not in terms of our earthly existence but in terms of the ultimate and eternal. Their impact must not be weakened. This means that the question of whether the demands of Jesus can in fact be fulfilled cannot be given a direct answer. To live from the power of God's new world is what really matters. And the only way in which this can be done is to expose ourselves to the new and to witness to it, having no concern for the consequences which this might involve.

VI

The discussion of our theme would not be complete without a closer examination of one basic element in the discipleship-tradition which up to this point has been dealt with only incidentally, and that is the commissioning of the disciples. The commission of Jesus to Peter and Andrew is that they are to become 'fishers of men'. One might object to this on the grounds that this commission is given to two of Jesus' best-known disciples and therefore constitutes an exception. Nevertheless, the saying is of quite fundamental importance.

We know from the Gospels that Jesus sent his disciples out. And just as we have to distinguish between the 'Twelve' and the 'disciples' before proceeding any farther, we must take note of a few more important factors in relation to the history of the tradition. For those belonging to the period in which the Gospels were written[36] the spreading of the Gospel was understood to be the task of the Twelve alone. Even Mark, who understands the disciples as a fairly wide and open group, describes only the Twelve as having a permanent life-relationship to Jesus and limits the mission to this Twelve.[37] Despite the fact that Matthew has adapted material from different traditions he nevertheless identifies the disciples with the Twelve. For him this is the only possible understanding and it is expressed most clearly in the missionary charge to the

28

Twelve in chapter 10. The Lukan account is different. In Luke 9 : 1ff., which is dependent upon Mark 6 : 7ff., there is the account of the sending out of the Twelve. But alongside this a different tradition is preserved according to which Jesus sends out a larger group of disciples, (Luke 10 : 1-16). Quite clearly the number seventy has an obvious symbolic significance and the parallel accounts of the two missions are meant to portray in advance the later activity of the disciples among the tribes of Israel and among the Gentiles. But the material on which Luke 10 is based, the so-called Logia-source,[38] makes it quite clear that Jesus' commission was not limited to the Twelve but that a much larger group was involved.[39] One might be led to have second thoughts as to the historicity of the mission as it is reported in the Gospels. There are certainly some grounds for doubts of this kind because traces of the missionary practice and experience of the early community are to be found in the missionary charges. Nevertheless, the fact that the disciples received a pre-Easter commission cannot be disputed.[40]

In order to grasp the biblical understanding of mission it must first of all be pointed out that it is not just a question of someone being sent out to another place with a special task. It means rather that being sent is something which requires a very definite kind of authorisation. A saying from the contemporary Jewish tradition runs as follows: 'The emissary of a man is just like the man who sent him'.[41] Here this is expressed as a principle, but the same idea is already to be found in the Old Testament in different forms.[42] For our purposes the mission of the prophets[43] is of particular interest because for one thing, their mission is not temporary but permanent, and secondly, their mission has to do with the proclamation of a message of either salvation or condemnation, and in Isaiah 61 : 1 the mission is even expressly connected with the proclamation of the eschatological good news.[44]

The prophets receive their commission directly from God. Correspondingly, in the New Testament, this is also true of Jesus.[45] What is decisive for our theme is the fact that Jesus hands on the commission which had been given to him to his disciples. This explains the saying in Luke 10 : 16: 'He who hears you hears me, and he who rejects you rejects me, and he who rejects me rejects him who sent me'. The sending out of the disciples rests upon the sovereign authority of Jesus, an authority which has been bestowed upon him and which he in turn confers and hands on. Therefore the mission of the disciples is just as inseparable from his person as discipleship itself. But it is equally true that a disciple can be the full representative of his master. And this helps to clarify the very surprising saying in Matt. 10 : 24ff: 'A disciple is not above his teacher, nor a servant above his master; it is enough for the disciple to be like his teacher, and the servant like his master'. The fact that a disciple is not above his master means that his authority is mediated and that he is always bound to the person of Jesus. On the other hand, he can become like his master, and this means that he may represent his Lord in the fullest sense. Discipleship is thus characterised by this peculiar subordination of the disciple to his master and yet at the same time by being his equal in the service to which he is called.

Luke 9 : 2 gives a brief indication of what the disciples are authorised to do: 'He (Jesus) sent them out to preach the kingdom of God and to heal'. Matt. 10 : 7 puts it in more concrete terms: 'And preach as you go, saying, "The kingdom of heaven is at hand". Heal the sick, raise the dead, cleanse lepers, cast out demons.'[46] This means that the disciples are given the same tasks which Jesus himself exercises as authorised by God. The disciple is equal to his master to such an extent that in principle the commission does not exclude him from doing what the master himself does. Therefore the disciples receive their commission and the promise to them is that they may share in the eschatological service of their master.[47]

Like Jesus himself, the disciples are called upon to gather together a new people of God. There can be no doubt that Jesus had no intention of forming a holy remnant[48] like some of the other contemporary Jewish groups,[49] but that from the very beginning his ministry was aimed at Israel as a whole. Nevertheless, despite the fact that his ministry concerned the Jews, he quite consciously crossed the boundaries of the old Israel and in one or two cases personally accepted the Gentiles.[50] This is because the coming of the kingdom of God, with its universal horizon, brought salvation for all men. Thus when the mission to the Gentiles got properly under way after Easter, and only then after serious discussions about its validity, it had nevertheless already been prepared for in the ministry of Jesus. The aim was therefore not to restore the old people of God but to call together a new people of God in view of God's imminent eschatological salvation.

This explains why Jesus appointed the Twelve.[51] They were not chosen for their task in order that they should be primarily and exclusively missionaries.[52] Rather, like the leaders of the twelve tribes of Israel they were chosen to be representatives of the new eschatological community. Nor did Jesus 'call' these Twelve to this task. (The call is a call to discipleship only.) He 'appointed' them, (Mark 3 : 14f.).[53] The Twelve lead the new people of God, and around this inner circle the disciples gather to await the consummation of salvation.

The question is often asked as to whether Jesus founded a 'church'. This must be answered with a decisive no. To pose the question in such a way is in any case quite wrong. And to assume that the community of the disciples understood itself as a church is something which cannot be established in terms of the pre-Easter history. What we understand by 'church', beginnings of which are already to be found in the New Testament, actually goes back to the concept of the *ekklesia* and its various developments. The earlier uses of this concept in the New Testament refer to the idea of the people of God. This is the sense in which it is used in the Greek translation of the Old Testament, the so-called Septuagint. Although the use of this term in early Christianity does not depend upon the Septuagint the same meaning is presupposed. This is because Jesus adopted traditions which were continued by the early church. These traditions made a terminological distinction between the people of God and the sects, i.e., the holy remnant. Therefore we cannot disregard that fact that the early Christian concept of the church is in certain respects strongly influenced by the idea of the gathering of the people of God.[54] Jesus is exclusively concerned that wherever the new kingdom of God is actualised, the new people of God should also gather. Other aspects of the *ekklesia* concept cannot be discussed here.

So far the basic characteristics of pre-Easter discipleship have been discussed. However, there can be no doubt that with the death and resurrection of Jesus there came certain deep and far-reaching changes. The fact that God had acted in Jesus provided a new and more profound knowledge of all that had gone before. Therefore a different and stronger emphasis than previously is now placed upon the Person of Jesus Christ. His pre-Easter activity could now be understood only in the light of Easter, and the message of the coming kingdom of God also became the message of Christ's death and resurrection.

The call to discipleship nevertheless lost none of its validity. And this is why the sayings and the events of the pre-Easter period were handed down as narratives in a fixed literary form. They were regarded not as having a merely historical reference, but as serving the actual proclamation. They became examples of what it meant to become and to be a Christian, and this explains their tendency to typify. The idea of the life-relationship to the master also had to be understood in a different way. This is where the living presence of the risen Christ becomes of such decisive importance. A saying such as Matt. 23 : 8, that there is one master and that no one can take his place, now received its full significance.[55]

The understanding of discipleship in the light of the Easter-event must be the subject of a separate study. Only then will it also become clear how the idea and concept of the church came to be developed. In preparation for what is to follow I should like to draw your attention to two texts:

(a) At the beginning, reference was made to the call of Peter. But this was dealt with only in relation to the story in Mark 1 : 16-18, (par. Matt. 4 : 18-20). Luke however, gives a considerably different account, (Luke 5 : 1-11). At first sight there appear to be even further complications because John 21 contains a similar story which is related to the Easter tradition. Nevertheless, with the help of John 21 we can understand Luke 5 better. In John 21 : 1-14 the report of the miraculous catch of fish is closely related to an appearance of the risen Jesus. In the traditional part of the story used by Luke fragments of Mark 1 : 16ff. and of John 21 : 1ff. can be recognised. Thus in Luke 5 the call of Peter which took place during the earthly ministry of Jesus is described along with the Easter encounter in a quite remarkable way, so that the two stories are seen as one.[56] This means in fact that the post-Easter community understood the call of Peter by the earthly Jesus in the light of this Easter commission. Thus he who was once called by Jesus was at the same time the one who was confirmed and authorised by the risen Jesus. This points to the theme which will be discussed in the following chapter.

(b) The second text relates to what will be discussed in the final chapter. The text is Matt. 16 : 18f., according to which Jesus says to Peter: 'You are Peter, and on this rock I will build my church, and the powers of death shall not prevail against it. I will give you the keys of the kingdom of heaven, and whatever you bind on earth shall be bound in heaven, and whatever you loose on earth shall be loosed in heaven.' The form in which the saying is presented here shows that it does not come from Jesus himself. It is based, however, on the incident when Simon[57] was given the name 'Peter'. It is most likely that this took place before Easter. It is also based upon the authorisation of the disciples to forgive sins. Why Simon was originally called 'Peter' cannot be stated with any certainty. It is possible that he received this name because he was the first disciple to be called. It has already been noted that the authority to forgive sins is closely related to Jesus' own activity. The exclusively rabbinic form in which this is stated here means however that it cannot be a saying of Jesus. Nevertheless the decisive thing about Matt 16 : 18f. is its overall intention and when we take this into account we can see that this saying is undeniably part of the proclamation of the post-Easter community. Thus even if we leave aside the special rôle of Peter and his power to bind and to loose, there are still a great number of differences to be noted in comparison with what we have discussed so far. For one thing the Greek word *ekklesia* here no longer denotes the people of God. There can be no doubt that it has taken on the meaning of 'community' or 'church'. This is particularly connected with the fact that the church is now seen as differentiated from the reign of God. And we have to say that a quite emphatic distinction is now made between the church and the *kingdom* of

God which is to be consummated in the future. Therefore it is not now a question of the new people of God gathering to await the coming reign of God. Rather, the church itself is, as it were, the present form of the reign of God, while the central motif of Jesus' preaching, namely, the kingdom of God, is here limited to the future consummation alone. This means that in this passage we have the beginnings of an 'ecclesiology', or an independent doctrine of the church. This presupposes considerable further development and further theological reflection.

The discussion of these problems is not part of my task. But they will be examined in more detail in the chapters which are to follow.

Notes to

PRE-EASTER DISCIPLESHIP

1. Cf. Ferdinand Hahn, Wenzel Lohff, Günther Bornkamm, *Die Frage nach dem historischen Jesus*, Evangelisches Forum, 2, Second ed. 1966. (Eng. Trans.: *What Can We Know About Jesus?* The Saint Andrew Press, 1969.)

2. In the time of Jesus one differentiated between bearers of the same name (i.e. christian name), by using the name of the father or by adding the name of his birthplace, an example of the latter is 'Jesus of Nazareth'.

3. Cf. Matt. 11 : 16-19, especially verse 19, and the parallel in Luke 7 : 31-34, especially verse 34.

4. The Markan text as we have it gives 1 : 16 as follows: 'And passing along by the Sea of Galilee. . . .' The phrase 'by the Sea of Galilee' is an editorial addition of the Evangelist and is not part of the original.

5. The image of the fisher of men is to be found in Jer. 16 : 16, Ezek. 47 : 10, and in rabbinic texts as well as in other places in ancient literature, but is always used in a sense which is meant to convey persuasion and deceit. Of course we cannot exclude the possibility that it may also have a positive meaning, but for this we lack references. However, here, it is most likely that the offensive meaning is taken up.

6. For the general reader, see Günther Bornkamm, *Jesus of Nazareth*, Hodder and Stoughton, 1960, pp. 144ff.; Eduard Lohse, Article: "Nachfolge Christi im Neuen Testament," in *Die Religion in Geschichte und Gegenwart*, Third ed., Vol. IV, cols. 1286-1288. For the more specialised reader: Articles by Gerhard Kittel and Karl-Heinrich Rengstorf in *Theological Dictionary of the New Testament*, Eerdmans, Vol. I, pp. 210-216; Vol. IV, pp. 390-461; also Eduard Schweizer, *Erniedrigung und Erhöhung bei Jesus und seinen Nachfolgern*, Second ed., 1962, esp. pp. 7ff.

(Eng. trans.: *Lordship and Discipleship*, SCM Studies in Biblical Theology, 1960, pp. 11ff.); the basic and detailed work of Anselm Schulz, *Nachfolgen und Nachahmen*, 1962; Hans Frh. von Campenhausen, *Tradition and Life in the Church*, Collins, 1968, esp. the essay "Early Christian Asceticism", pp. 90ff.; Georg Kretschmar, "Ein Beitrag zur Frage nach dem Ursprung der frü. christlichen Askese", *Zeitschrift für Theologie und Kirche* (Z.Th.K.), 61, 1964, pp. 27-67 and esp. pp. 49ff. Other works which may be consulted: Dietrich Bonhoeffer, *The Cost of Discipleship*, SCM Press, 1959; Karl Barth, *Church Dogmatics*, IV/2, pp. 533ff.

7. The content of the *imitatio* concept in the New Testament is determined by the idea of discipleship. In addition to the imitation of Christ (1 Thess. 1 : 6; 1 Cor. 11 : 1), there is also the imitation of the apostle, (1 Thess. 1 : 6; 2 Thess. 3 : 7, 9; 1 Cor. 4 : 16; 11 : 1; Phil. 3 : 17), and there is even a single instance which demands the imitation of God Himself, (Eph. 5 : 1). While with the idea of the imitation of Christ the emphasis is upon humility and obedience, with the imitation of God it is the readiness to forgive; but there is no question here of an ethic based upon God and Christ as examples. Where the imitation of the apostle is concerned, it means to emulate in faith and to be totally dependent on the Lord. For details cf. A. Schulz, op.cit., pp. 199ff.

8. See Reinhold Seeberg, "Die Nachfolge Christi", in *Aus Religion und Geschichte*, collected essays and lectures, Vol. 1, pp. 1-41; Erich Kähler, "Nachfolge Christi", in *Die Religion in Geschichte und Gegenwart*, Third ed., Vol. IV, cols. 1288-1292.

9. The idea of 'following God' is also of considerable importance in the Old Testament, but we shall show that the New Testament concept is not related to this idea. In this connection see Martin Buber's essay "Nachahmung Gottes" which was first published in 1925 and is now in the Collected Works, Vol. II, pp. 1053-1066, 1964.

10. Since the time of Ezra, the Law and its interpretation had become the centre of interest. It is for this reason that the tradition of scribal learning can be traced back to Ezra's time, (cf. Ezra 7 : 6, 11ff.).

11. In later times Jewish rabbis were ordained. It is difficult to determine when this practice was introduced; it probably became general practice after A.D. 70.

12. Cf. e.g. Hos. 2 : 1-17.

13. Cf. e.g. Jer. 7 : 9; 8 : 2, and 1 Kings 18 : 21.

14. In the Old Testament we hear more than once about groups of prophets, e.g. 1 Sam. 10 : 10ff.; we may certainly assume that disciples of the prophets were also present.

15. Most of the official prophets were 'cultic prophets' or 'salvation prophets', who were strongly attacked by e.g. Jeremiah, cf. Jer. 23 : 9ff.

16. German text according to the Zürich Bible, English from RSV.

17. Cf. the well-known example of Paul who as a Jewish rabbi had already learnt the trade of tentmaker, (Acts 18 : 3).

18. This in turn, especially in relation to Paul, also had far-reaching consequences for the understanding of a person's occupation (Beruf), which within the Christian context could be understood in the sense of a special 'calling' (Berufung); cf. Karl Holl, "Die Geschichte des Wortes

Beruf", in *Gesammelte Aufsätze zur Kirchengeschichte*, III, 1928, pp. 189-219.

19. A comparable state of affairs is to be found in the Old Testament and in Judaism but applied only to priests and Levites. Corresponding quotations from the Old Testament are occasionally given in the New Testament, (e.g. 1 Cor. 9 : 13). Nevertheless we must keep in mind that this principle is quite uncommon within the general discipleship tradition.

20. Cf. 1 Thess. 2: (3ff.) 9ff.; 1 Cor. 4 : 11f., 9 : 6ff. He adopted a different attitude towards the community at Philippi, cf. Phil. 4 : 10ff.

21. The older form of the story is to be found in Mark. Matthew is the one who refers to a 'young man'.

22. H. von Campenhausen, op.cit. (*Tradition and Life in the Church*, p. 92).

23. We possess this promise in its later, more extended form where the reference is to the Christian brotherhood and its sharing of possessions 'with persecutions'. The version given above probably corresponds more closely to the original.

24. In Mark 8 : 35 and parallels, the phrase 'and the gospel's' is probably a later addition. It may even be asked whether 'for my sake' is also secondary. This saying of Jesus may originally have included the phrase which Luke gives: 'for the sake of the kingdom of God', (Luke 18 : 29).

25. Here as in Mark 8 : 35 the Greek word is 'psyche', which in our German translations of the Bible is usually rendered *Seele* (soul). (Translator's note: Older English translations also translate as 'soul'.) This actually corresponds to the Old Testament *nephesh*, which does not mean the soul as distinct from the body, but the life which God gives and which makes physical existence possible. The concept 'psyche' therefore denotes the life of a person as it manifests itself in terms of the whole of his personal existence.

26. For more details about the problems of this Logion, see Erich Dinkler's essay, "Jesu Wort vom Kreuztragen", in *Neutestamentliche Studien für Rudolf Bultmann, Beiheft zur Zeitschrift für neutestamentliche Wissenschaft und die Kunde der älteren Kirche (BZNW)* 21, Second ed., 1957, pp. 110-129. He suggests that this saying was originally an instance of a declaration of ownership. This would then mean that the disciple would belong completely to his Lord and so must share his destiny.

27. The question concerning those titles which may go back directly to Jesus or which were at least originated by him can be left aside. There is no doubt that, as we find them in the New Testament, their function is to interpret the early Christian proclamation-theology.

28. The significant thing here are the parallel statements about the time which is fulfilled and the imminent kingdom of God. It is in this way that the remarkable tension between present and future is expressed. For precisely this reason the Greek phrase, 'the kingdom of God is at hand' should not be understood in the sense that the kingdom is indeed temporally near but still to come. Sayings such as Luke 11 : 20 (par. Matt. 12 : 28) state that the kingdom of God, understood in terms of Jesus'

activity, 'has come upon you'. The background to Mark 1 : 15 in the Aramaic means a coming which already reaches into the present though without cancelling its futurity. It refers therefore to an advent of salvation, the completion of which is yet to come, cf. Günther Bornkamm, *Jesus of Nazareth*, pp. 64ff. The present form of the phrase in Mark 1 : 15 'and believe in the gospel' with its definitive understanding of 'gospel' and its demand to 'believe' in this gospel can be traced back to the proclamation-language of the early church. However, this does not exclude the fact that Jesus understood himself as the messenger of salvation whose mission it was to proclaim the eschatological good news. Cf. Matt. 11 : 5, par. Luke 7 : 22. The background to this is the Old Testament tradition, in Is. 52 : 7; 61 : 1.

29. It would be a mistake to trivialize Jesus' uncompromising criticism of the Old Testament and of the current religious ordinances of Judaism. When he is understood as having come not to abolish but to fulfil the Law and the prophets, (Matt. 5 : 17), it should not be taken to mean that he submits himself to the exact letter of the Old Testament. This can already be seen from the antitheses of the Sermon on the Mount. A saying such as Matt. 5 : 18, according to which neither an iota nor a dot will pass from the Law is not a genuine saying of Jesus. This is rather an example of the way in which early Christianity tended to re-introduce Jewish ideas. Matthew is the only Evangelist who takes account of specifically Jewish-Christian traditions. However, generally speaking, he does not moderate the radical nature of Jesus' Word in order to make allowances for the particularistic tendencies of these circles.

30. This is preceded by the saying about 'hating' one's own family and the saying about taking up the cross, (Luke 14 : 26f.).

31. Mark uses the terms 'disciples' and 'Twelve', but he does not equate the two. In Mark 6 : 30 he refers to 'apostles', but this is only casual and without emphasis. Luke quite consistently equates the 'Twelve' with the 'apostles', but according to 1 Cor. 15 : 5f. this cannot be historically true. He does however distinguish the wider circle of 'disciples' from the 'Twelve' and the 'apostles'. Matthew on the other hand especially aims at identifying the 'disciples' and the 'Twelve' because for him the 'Twelve disciples' are the representatives of the Christian community. He also identifies the 'Twelve disciples' with the 'apostles' but for Matthew this is only of secondary importance.

32. This is a term which is derived from Form-Criticism, a method which examines the pre-literary stage of the tradition. Cf. Martin Dibelius, *Jesus*, SCM Press, 1963, pp. 13ff. For further reference see his more detailed work, *Die Formgeschichte des Evangeliums*, Fourth ed., 1961, p. 34ff.

33. Cf. Dietrich Bonhoeffer, *Ethics*, SCM Press, 1960, pp. 84ff.

34. In the history of theology the view has often been put forward that the demands of the Sermon on the Mount can in no way be fulfilled, but rather serve as a mirror held up to man's sin. This view gives only a partial explanation of their real meaning. For the history of the interpretation of the Sermon on the Mount, cf. Günther Bornkamm, *Jesus of Nazareth*, pp. 221ff.

35. There are traces of this to be found in Matt. 18, but this is based on a later collection and interpretation of the sayings of Jesus.

36. Mark is the oldest Gospel, written *circa* A.D. 70. Matthew and Luke may be dated between A.D. 80 and A.D. 90, and John probably in the early nineties.

37. Mark 3 : 14f.; 6 : 7-13, 30.

38. The 'Logia-source' ('Q') has been worked into the Gospels of Matthew and Luke along with the Markan account. Matthew has clearly broken up the sequence of the Logia-source in order to arrange it to his own style of composition. The original sequence is to a certain extent recognizable in the Lukan account.

39. This is related to the fact that in the early period after Easter a clear distinction was made between the Twelve and the Apostles, (cf. 1 Cor. 15 : 5f.).

40. More detailed grounds for this assumption are given in my book, *Das Verständnis der Mission im Neuen Testament*, Second ed. 1965, pp. 19ff. (Eng. trans.: *Mission in the New Testament*, SCM Studies in Biblical Theology, 1965, pp. 26ff.).

41. Mishna, Berachoth; 5 : 5.

42. E.g. in the realm of constitutional law in relation to a delegation, (e.g. 2 Sam. 10 : 1ff.), or in the sphere of private law in relation to the legal act of engagement, or divorce, or a purchase.

43. Cf. e.g. the story of the call of Isaiah, (6 : 8).

44. These are the presuppositions for the New Testament use of the verb *apostellein* and in an indirect way for the later titular use of the word *apostolos*. This is clearly seen in Luke 4 : 26; 11 : 49; 13 : 34, par. Matt. 23 : 37; Mark 12 : 2, 4, 5. The 'Shaliach-Office' of the Jewish central authorities in Jerusalem is of no importance in this respect. This is because this office issued only temporary commissions limited to administrative purposes, and which had nothing to do with preaching or teaching. There is certainly no hint of its having had an eschatological or missionary function. The origins of the Jewish Shaliach-Office can nevertheless be traced back to the tra litional understanding of mission.

45. Cf. the closely related sayings, Mark 9 : 37, par. Luke 9 : 48; Luke 10 : 16, par. Matt 10 : 40, and John 13 : 20. In John's Gospel the sending of the Son by the Father is frequently mentioned, cf. e.g. 3 : 17; 8 : 42; 10 : 36; 12 : 44f. See also Gal. 4 : 4; Rom. 8 : 3.

46. Cf. Mark 6 : 7, 13f.; Luke 10 : (8), 9, 11b.

47. The fact that the disciples can also fail to fulfil their task can be seen from Mark 9 : 14-30 and par.

48. This conception is based on I Kings 19 : 18 and upon the promise of Isaiah, see 1 : 8f.; 6 : 13; 7 : 3; 10 : 20-23.

49. This is especially true of the Pharisees and of the Qumran community.

50. Cf. Mark 7 : 24-30, par. Matt. 15 : 21-28; Matt. 8 : 5-13, par. Luke 7 : 1-10.

51. The appointment of the Twelve prior to Easter has always been the subject of debate. My own view is however that unless one reckons with the fact that the earthly Jesus did appoint the Twelve, it is impossible

to understand the part played by Judas, the early history of Palestinian Christianity and the formation of the whole tradition concerning the Twelve.

52. This was also the case in the post-Easter period when the Twelve were resident in Jerusalem most of the time. Peter, however, dedicated himself more and more to the work of mission.

53. In Mark 3 : 16-19 a list follows giving the names of the Twelve; cf. Matt. 10 : 2-4; Luke 6 : 14-16; Acts 1 : 13. The names in these lists are in most cases the same. However there are variations, e.g. James, the son of Alphaeus, is called Matthew in the first Gospel, cf. Matt. 9 : 9 where he alters Mark 2 : 14. In addition Luke refers to a second Simon instead of Thaddaeus, (Luke 6 : 15; Acts 1 : 13).

54. Cf. especially Gal. 6 : 16b; 1 Peter 2 : 9f.; Heb. 3 : 7-4 : 11; the idea of the New Covenant is also to be seen in this framework: 1 Cor. 11 : 25; 2 Cor. 3 : 7-18; Heb. 8 : 6, 9 : 15-22, 10 : 15-18, 12 : 24. It should also be noted that modern research questions the derivation of the *ekklesia* concept from the Old Testament and Jewish idea of the people of God.

55. It is most likely that this is a post-Easter saying of the Lord proclaimed to the community through prophets. Such circumstances therefore serve to intensify its meaning.

56. I take a different view of this from the one put forward by Günter Klein at the 'Kirchentag' in Cologne in 1965, (see Günter Klein, Willi Marxsen, Walter Kreck, *Bibelkritik und Gemeindefrömmigkeit*, 1966, pp. 11-31. Luke (5 : 1-13) has also taken account of Jesus' sermon at the lakeside. He has not reduced the immediacy of the call to discipleship, though the fishermen kept mending (washing) their nets during the sermon and paid no attention to it.

57. This incident is handed down independently of Matt. 16 : 18f.; cf. Mark 3 : 16, par. Luke 6 : 14; John 1 : 42.

Discipleship in the Light of the Easter-event

By AUGUST STROBEL

THIS chapter will involve the very basic problem of faith in its relation to historical criticism. Most of us whose background to faith is provided by the church have a natural shyness about questioning the Easter texts in a critical way. We are afraid lest something should happen to the truth which is expressed in these texts. We have the feeling that this truth might be destroyed and are apprehensive when it comes to putting the Easter texts to any critical test. But in fact an attitude like this endangers the Christian message of Easter more than any critical approach which is itself aware of its own limits and responsibilities. If we are to speak about an Easter-event (and this is what our theme requires us to do), then we cannot relieve others nor ourselves of the responsibility of determining its content. We consider it legitimate to test any event in our contemporary world by means of critical methods and we try if possible to find solutions. If we regard the Easter-event in terms of this wider context then our questions about the beginnings and the structures of discipleship in the light of Easter will find an appropriate answer.

I. *The Easter-event and the Witness of Easter*

1. *What does the New Testament say?*

Even the most unversed readers can see that the New Testament reports differ. In 1 Cor. 15 Paul refers to an appearance of Jesus to Peter, to the Twelve (or the Eleven?), to more than 500 brethren, to James the brother of the Lord, and to 'all' the apostles. This last was probably to a wider circle of helpers who are not simply to be equated with the Twelve. Last in this list of witnesses comes Paul himself when he tells us that Jesus appeared to him also. All in all, this list of witnesses, which is the oldest we possess, comprises of about 550 people who could claim to have had an authentic experience. This figure does not necessarily fit our idea of the Easter-event. Paul, who is writing approximately twenty years after the ministry of Jesus was completed, obviously still feels the impact of these overwhelming events. In a similar way, the traditional material which has been used in Acts 1 : 3ff., stresses the 'many proofs' by which the risen Christ presented himself to his disciples.

The Testimony of the *Gospels* clearly differs from this. They all refer to the empty tomb, and in their description of how it was discovered by the women, they mention either one angel or two as providing the first news about what had happened. The Gospels apparently do not presuppose a large number of appearances or of Easter-witnesses. Compared with Paul's list above, what the Gospels have to offer is distinctly meagre. At first sight, Mark, the oldest Gospel, which breaks off abruptly at 16 : 8, seems to offer no help at all. However, a hint seems to be given that Jesus revealed himself to the disciples in Galilee. Matthew, (28 : 1-20), describes the appearance of Jesus to the women by the graveside, but apart from this he mentions only the appearance to the Eleven on a mountain in Galilee. Although Matthew's purpose is to make no mention of the ascension he does not even try to compensate for this by giving accounts of other appearances. Luke, (24 : 1-53), casually reports a first appearance to Peter. There is the very full account of the two disciples on the road to Emmaus. Finally, there is an account of an appearance of Jesus to the Eleven, around whom a wider group of disciples had gathered (24 : 33). On the same Easter Sunday, when they had gone out to a place near Bethany, Jesus is said to have been taken up into heaven. John speaks about an appearance to Mary Magdalene and of an appearance to the disciples apart from Thomas on Easter Sunday, then again of an appearance to the disciples eight days later, this time Thomas being present. According to John, the actual commissioning of the disciples took place on the evening of Easter Sunday, as with Luke. In the appendix (chapter 21), which does not originally belong to John's Gospel, another, so-called 'third' appearance to seven disciples by the Sea of Tiberias is described. The leading figure in this group is Peter, and the background to this passage is probably the pre-Johannine single account of the first call of Peter. The so-called 'inauthentic' ending of Mark (16 : 9-20), which in fact was never intended to be 'authentic' at all, but which was added at the beginning of the second century in order to round off this unfinished Gospel, enumerates a 'first' appearance to Mary Magdalene, (cf. Matt. 28 : 9f.; John 20 : 11ff.), then another to two disciples, (cf. Luke : 24 : 13ff.), and lastly an appearance to the Eleven during a meal, (Luke 24 : 36ff.; John 20 : 19ff.). After this it is said that Jesus ascended into heaven. (This means that according to this sequence the ascension must have taken place in Jerusalem.)

This review of the material shows that according to the Evangelists only a very small group of disciples were involved in witnessing the Easter-event. They lack the long list of witnesses which Paul brings forward as evidence. Taking into account the numerous inner contradictions as regards the place, the time and the mode of the appearances, it is almost impossible to talk about 'the light of the Easter-event' at all. Thus it looks as though any attempt which sets out to show how the disciples re-grouped and how they understood themselves anew in this event is faced with problems which are almost insoluble. This being the case, we must try to make the historical context clearer.

2. *What is the Position of Modern Research?*

During the past few decades the problem to which New Testament research has addressed itself is not so much the historical problem as such, but the very closely related question of the literary and narrative form of the Easter stories.[1] Is it not the case that the Easter stories and the Easter faith which is expressed in them take on typical forms? On the one hand we read about the appearances of angels at the empty tomb, on the other, of appearances of Christ in different places. In a stereotyped way the stories describe the fear and doubts of the women, or the unbelief and doubts of the disciples whenever they catch a glimpse of the risen Christ. He discloses himself to them by speaking to them. This is followed by either words of instruction or of promise. Then in most cases there follows the decisive commissioning to new service. The fixed pattern of these reports is either traditional, (cf. the Old Testament accounts of the calling of the prophets, or of appearances of God or of angels), or is partly derived from the contemporary background, (e.g., the hellenistic undertones in Mark 16 : 5 when he speaks about 'a young man', whereas Matt. 28 : 2 refers to 'an angel of the Lord'). The literary form into which these stories have been moulded also means that they very often lack the note of immediate experience, (e.g., Matt. 28 : 17). But at the same time this fixed pattern acted as a necessary practical aid to contemporary readers. It gave expression to the action of God which the first disciples had experienced in an illustrative and easily understandable way. The theological intention of these reports is therefore quite clear. It was not that the disciples themselves thought these things up, rather they were taken into these events despite the fact that due to everything that had happened they had not deserved it, (e.g., the betrayal by Judas, the denials of Peter and of all the others). Therefore the stereotyped literary form of the Easter stories rightly present the disciples as sinful men who are frightened and who doubt once more, yet at the same time they are presented as men who are pardoned, and as those to whom God's new reality has been overwhelmingly disclosed. Modern research has made the discovery that in these stories the witness of faith is of more importance than historical detail. To assert that these stories are exact historical reports is a statement which would require further consideration. Nevertheless, the efforts of modern research are not entirely fruitless. This situation justifies the various attempts to reconstruct the course of events. But just because these are attempts at reconstruction, findings are provisional and hypothetical.

We must first of all mention the radical interpretation of E. Hirsch,[2] who refers quite consistently to the Easter stories as 'legends'. He asserts that these stories are the result of the poetic and religious imagination of the first Christians who were motivated by a profound eschatological belief in eternal life. He holds that 1 Cor. 15 is more trustworthy than the Gospel reports. He suggests that the discovery of the empty tomb by the women on Easter morning is most probably historically true. They fled in fear and at first kept quiet about their discovery. According to Hirsch, it is likely that the oldest tradition made no reference to angels at the graveside. As for the disciples, they had already fled to Galilee when they had found themselves confronted with the catastrophe of Jesus' death. Having taken up their former occupations they became convinced on the strength of visionary experiences that their Lord had ascended to God and had been appointed the coming Lord and Christ. It was because of a vision, says Hirsch, that Peter was the first to become certain of this. Later, this certainty spread to the Twelve with the help of Peter. Eventually they all returned to Jerusalem, where, according to the belief of the day, the expected Messiah must be proclaimed. At Pentecost more than 500 followers of Jesus fell into an ecstatic trance. Finally, Jesus' relatives were also caught up in the tumult of the new faith. In the course of another gathering of ecstatic believers a wider circle of apostles came to the decision that the whole of Israel should be won over. E. Hirsch can therefore be regarded as a typical representative of the so-called subjective visions theory. The origins of the post-Easter community of disciples are understood as being rooted in a psychological-visionary chain-reaction. According to this view, Easter is something which has been produced by people who were certainly believers, but who were primarily visionaries.[3]

Unlike E. Hirsch, Hans Grass[4] does not want to relate the Easter message to two historical facts: i.e., to the empty tomb *and* to visionary experiences. Grass regards the story of the empty tomb as unhistorical. Paul knows nothing of the empty tomb nor does he show any special interest in it. For Paul, the question of the whereabouts of the physical body was quite secondary. This was because he had a much more radical understanding of the risen body than his Jewish contemporaries who held that the old and the new had to be identical. Grass goes on to say that as with the stories which describe the finding of the empty tomb, the accounts of the appearances in Jerusalem are also unhistorical. Presumably it was only in Galilee that Peter had a decisive experience. Like Hirsch, Grass works with the theory that the disciples fled to Galilee. This, however, is not entirely supported by the texts. A further appearance to the Eleven made them return to Jerusalem, (probably for Pentecost[5]). At the same time they all realised that their commission was to proclaim the risen Christ. 'Like the Master before the feast of the Passover the disciples must have disturbed Jerusalem with their un-precedented message.'[6] As for the appearances themselves Grass describes them as 'objective visions'. In this way Grass tries to give adequate expression to the difference between the imagination of the individual disciples who shared in these appearances, and the independent nature of the visions themselves, the latter being a point which the stories repeatedly stress. Grass concludes that a theological interpretation has no grounds for questioning the visionary character of early Christianity. He also maintains that this does not mean that the disciples had simply deluded themselves.[7] In the critical view of Grass, Easter doubtlessly remains the event accom-plished by God. And it is in terms of this event that the disciples re-thought their calling and started out anew on the road to what was to become the church.

In contrast to Grass, Hans von Campenhausen,[8] for historical and exegetical reasons, takes the view that we must regard the empty tomb as a quite definite historical fact. In contrast to those who hold the theory that the disciples fled, he states that after their movement had collapsed the disciples did not immediately flee to Galilee. In accordance with all the Gospel reports, he says, it is more likely that they at first stayed in Jerusalem, and there their mood was one of depres-sion, fear and perplexity. The women's news about the empty tomb roused them, but (according to Mark and Luke), it seems that no appearance of Christ took place at first. It is quite possible that Peter was the first to understand the empty tomb as a sign that the resurrection had taken place, (cf. Luke). He then led the others to Galilee, (cf. Mark, Matthew and the Gospel of Peter), because they hoped to meet Jesus there as they had been told: 'There you will see him', (Mark 16 : 7, cf. Mark 14 : 28). In passing, von Campenhausen weighs up the possibility that the hope of the disciples was originally directed not only to meeting Jesus again but to the Parousia[9] (the return of the Lord at the end of time). However, he concludes that the account as it has come down to us no longer gives any evidence of this possibility. As far as von Campenhausen is concerned the appearances reported by Paul in 1 Cor. 15 could have happened in Galilee. On the other hand, it is possible that the appearances to James and to the other apostles could have taken place in Jerusalem, the centre of the early church. It was only much later that Jesus appeared to Paul, and in any case this is a different matter. What can we say then about the whereabouts of the body of Jesus? Von Campenhausen's opinion is that this question allows the imagination a wide range of possibilities.[10] Nevertheless, no matter what kind of answer one may nowadays give to this particular question, faith in the bodily resurrection of Jesus can remain basically unshaken. Faith knows that 'this is a remarkable event in every sense', an event 'with which the new Aeon begins and in which the old world with its laws comes to an end'. Hans von Campenhausen obviously makes a clear distinction between what is possible historically and what cannot be surrendered theologically.[11]

The main historical problems of the Easter-event can be shown in terms of these three different views.[12] They deal with the problems of the 'empty tomb', 'the flight of the disciples' to Galilee, the question of whether the appearances took place in Jerusalem or in Galilee, and the problem of who was the first to have a visionary experience (Peter and the Eleven, or the women). In any attempt to solve these problems it is always necessary to weigh up the evidence of the Gospel reports and to compare this with 1 Cor. 15. It is from the Gospel reports that we reconstruct the course of events on Easter morning as best we can. But we rely on the oldest list of witnesses (1 Cor. 15) with regard to the question of the later sequences of the most important appearances. However, there is hardly any need to emphasise that this harmonising method has its short-comings. Simply to determine the value or the lack of value of any one story is not sufficient. Therefore it is necessary to find out the laws of development behind the individual traditions and also the intentions which have shaped their composition. This procedure does not permit us to give free rein to our imagination in dealing with the dark period of the pre-history of the Gospel material. Rather, the laws according to which this material has developed help us to come to more convincing conclusions about the original event. Just how promising this method is may be seen from the studies which have centred upon 1 Cor. 15 : 3ff.

3. *What is the Position of Research with regard to the Oldest List of Witnesses?*

The more recent contributions to this passage concentrate on distinguishing the different traditions which Paul has used and on tracing their origins. P. Winter,[13] like others before him,[14] was of the opinion that two different lists had been worked into this passage: a Jewish-Christian tradition with Peter as the central figure, (the witnesses are Peter, the Twelve and the 500), and another Jewish-Christian tradition with James as the central figure, (the witnesses being James and 'all the apostles'). He holds that these different lists reflect the rivalry of two early Christian groups. One of these groups was committed to the moderate party of Peter, and the other to the radical party of James. According to U. Wilckens[15] Paul has combined material from a kerygmatic tradition with material from a catechetical tradition, (cf. v. 3f. and vv. 5-7). He also distinguishes between two traditions which were originally parallel: one concerning Cephas and the Twelve (v. 5), the other concerning James and the apostles (v. 7). Verse 6, which is more narrative in style than the others, and which refers to an appearance to more than 500 brethren, is said to come from Paul himself. According to Wilckens these traditions prior to Paul already hint at a shift of influence from Peter to James. On linguistic and on formal grounds the phases 'he appeared to Cephas, then to the Twelve', go back to an old pre-Pauline 'confirmation-formula' (from the early history of the primitive community). Perhaps U. Wilckens makes too much of this. It is not just that certain disciples should be confirmed, but that the Christ-event should be confirmed. It is generally accepted that vv. 3b-5 is a well-defined and self-contained confession-formula[16] running as follows:

'Christ died for our sins in accordance with the scriptures, and was buried.

He was raised on the third day in accordance with the scriptures and appeared to Cephas, then to the Twelve.'

It is also widely recognised that this formula is older than its continuation in verses 6a and 7. Some studies conclude with the suggestion that the formula originated in the early Palestinian community.[17] Against this view there is Eduard Schweizer[18] who does not attach much importance to the Semitisms which are said to support this thesis on the grounds that these can also be traced to the Greek and could well have been influenced by the Septuagint. He is also right in pointing out that the formula puts the emphasis on the death of Jesus, the saving significance of which is confirmed by the resurrection. Similarly, Ph. Vielhauer[19] points out that the content of the formula, e.g., with reference to the sacrificial death of Jesus (cf. 'for'), might well have been derived from Palestinian Judaism. But according to Vielhauer it is more likely that because of the way in which these verses are formulated, they go back to a Jewish-Christian Hellenistic context.

Hans Conzelmann,[20] who also reckons that the theology of the formula is pre-Pauline, traces it more specifically to a confession-formula of the Antiochene community. He says that this provides us with an insight into the founding of the church and that it may be connected with the first appearance of the risen Christ to Peter. But how are we to explain the appearance to the Twelve who first of all had to be brought together again? Conzelmann is of the opinion that Peter interpreted the appearance to himself as a call to fulfil precisely this task. He thus became the centre of the new group of disciples because he had reunited the twelve representatives of the people of God. It is worth noting, says Conzelmann, that Paul's brief hint about Cephas and the Twelve has been enlarged to include the long list of witnesses given in 1 Cor. 15. Conzelmann tries to explain this with the theory that this does not merely indicate a quantitative extension in time, but that it points much more to a change in the understanding of time itself, (which had originally been understood in the strict eschatological sense). More and more, the era of the church begins to displace the creative eschatological moment.[21] This was done in order to provide a justification for the church.

It is clear at any rate that in 1 Cor. 15 various traditions concerning the appearances have been worked in. The older and most important tradition (v. 5b) testifies to the Easter experience of Peter and to the experience of the Twelve. Verse 6 probably reflects another independent tradition. However, it is most unlikely that this verse is a rival tradition going back to James and the apostles. Reasons for this are the specifically Pauline concept of apostle (v. 7), and the typically Pauline structure, (e.g., 'then,' 'then'; cf. e.g., 1 Cor. 15 : 23-24). This means that Paul has combined two other separate traditions which deal with the appearances. He probably had good reasons for mentioning his own vision of Christ after the appearance to 'all the apostles' so that it came last. By 'all the apostles' he probably meant a larger group of people who had been sent out to proclaim the Word.[22]

It is hardly likely that this group had already been constituted during the first few weeks after Easter. It was probably Paul's view that the Easter experiences were spread out over a period of one or two years. Such a length of time is certainly remarkable. Nevertheless one may still ask whether this really was meant to provide a theological justification for the so-called era of the church. What is more surprising is the fact that Paul assumed the existence of a large, almost unlimited number of Easter witnesses in the early stages. We catch a glimpse of the extent to which strong impulses went out from these early witnesses. And it is quite clear that there is a considerable difference between Paul's view and that of the Evangelists.

4. What Conclusions can we draw so far?

All the reports clearly maintain that something actually happened during and after Easter. The pre-Pauline tradition in 1 Cor. 15 : 3-5 represents an important testimony to an experience of Peter and of the Twelve. The attempts at reconstruction which we have outlined all hold to this and connect it with the original event. However, the details of the original event itself seem to be largely in darkness. The testimonies of the Gospels, in which the figure of Peter always stands out in one way or another, (Mark 16: 7; Luke 24: 34; John 20 : 6ff.; 21 : 15.; and Matt. 16 : 18f.), and which also agree in their reference to an appearance to the Eleven, (Mark 16 : 7 ; Luke 24 : 36ff.; Matt. 28 : 16ff.; John 20 : 19ff.;

Acts 1 : 4), can be regarded as firm support for the historical outline which we have just sketched.

Recently, the question has again been raised as to whether we may not in fact have more grounds for assuming that the original events took place in Jerusalem.[23] The flight of the disciples to Galilee remains an especially difficult problem in the whole sequence of events. The texts give only a vague hint of this and we are therefore compelled to deal with this problem in more detail. Meanwhile, it is sufficient to stress that so far there is obvious agreement about the fact that at Easter something actually took place. The differences between Paul and the Gospels pose a number of more difficult problems.[24] The Gospels limit the Easter-event to the women and to the inner circle of the disciples. They also confine it within the first few days or weeks. According to Luke and John, the decisive appearance occurred on Easter Sunday only. The Acts of the Apostles allow for the first forty days. But Paul differs entirely. His understanding of the Easter-event is much wider not only with regard to time, but also as regards those who witnessed it. Is it possible to clarify these problems further?

II. *The Easter-Witness and its Tradition*

Behind the testimony of the Gospels, which were written relatively late, there are definite intentions and laws according to which the traditions have been developed. This is a factor which must be taken into account. This provides us with an insight into the way in which the Easter faith had to defend itself against attack, and also to some extent into the origins of the Easter faith itself. Easter as something to be proclaimed with conviction, as is the case with Paul, and as something to be defended against doubts and misunderstandings, are two different things. On occasion one aspect of the event would be emphasised, on a different occasion another aspect for the sake of preserving the truth. What then are the principal laws behind the tradition which have determined the handing down of the Easter-witness?

1. *Clarification through Limitation.*

If our interpretation is correct, Paul's long list of witnesses and the longer period of time which he gives to the Easter-event is not to be understood as a theological justification for the era of the church. What is more important is that Paul belonged to a period when there was an abundance of traditions and witnesses. This is an indication of the incredible richness and variety of the different experiences. There can be no doubt that in the earliest period this is where the interest lay. This is not so much the case with the Evangelists who wrote towards the end of the first century, (Mark *circa* A.D. 70; Matt. and Luke between A.D. 70 and A.D. 90, and John *circa* A.D. 100). In contrast to Paul they show no interest in a large number of witnesses. They are more interested in the trustworthiness of the witnesses and in the origins of the event, the effects of which were still apparent in their own time. This means that the truth of the original event had to be their real concern. And again in contrast to Paul this meant that they had to concern themselves with the historical details. It goes without saying that for the sake of giving theological expression to the event, certain religious and theological motifs had to be incorporated. The messenger from heaven, for example, who reveals God's truth, has obvious biblical and contemporary parallels. According to the respective understanding or environment of the writer he is described as 'a young man' or as 'an angel', (cf. 2 Macc. 3 : 26, 33; and Jos. Ant. 5, 8, 2; the Gospel according to Peter 35ff.).[25] The significance of this figure is to be understood in terms of his function rather than his nature. It is his function to vouch for the knowledge of God and the action of God. He is the representative from the heavenly world who makes visible to the surprised and passive disciples the inbreaking of the divine and the beginning of something overwhelmingly new. We can see a general tendency to describe the full impact and reality of the Easter experience of the first disciples. Matthew gives an unusually detailed description of the miracle of the angel opening the grave. Luke and John refer to two messengers from heaven, for in accordance with contemporary beliefs two witnesses were required to confirm the truth, (Deut. 19 : 15; Is. 8 : 2). Another example of this is the account in which

Jesus is described as eating in the presence of the disciples to show that he was actually physically present, (Luke 24 : 41ff.; cf. also John 21 : 9ff. and Mark 16 : 14). Reports are also given which stress the fact that the living Lord permitted others to touch him, (Luke 24 : 39 and John 20 : 24ff.). Here it is worth noting that John, whose Gospel was the last to be written, shows a certain tendency to emphasise the exceptional nature of this demonstrative action. Only Thomas is granted the favour. Yet at the same time he is criticised for his lack of faith. The story of Jesus' appearance to Mary Magdalene comes to a significant climax when he turns her away with the words; 'Do not hold me', (20 : 17). Obviously John's main intention is to describe both the physical presence and the heavenly otherness of Jesus. His testimony is already directed against emphasising the spiritual at the expense of the physical and vice versa. At first his presentation appears to be contradictory. We have to remember however, that his intention is to protect the truth as he understands it from the extreme views of Judaism on the one hand and also from Hellenistic-Gnostic spiritualism on the other. John's aim is to clarify, and this in turn also influences the way in which he presents the historical details of the earliest sequence of events. But according to John the time taken up by the original sequence of events is strictly limited (despite the fact that the picture which he presents is extremely detailed). For Luke the whole series of events is limited to the Easter Sunday. It can be seen that John also stresses the Easter Sunday because this is the time when the disciples are given their commission and when they receive the Holy Spirit. Therefore we have to pay special attention to this way in which the Gospels tend to give detailed descriptions of the Easter events. At the same time, the view shared by the Gospels is that the period of time over which the events extended was very brief. Reference has already been made to this. Nevertheless, this is quite an important point for it helps us to recognise that it is perfectly possible that the Evangelists drew their information from dependable sources.[26]

Mark and Matthew emphasise that the revelatory event of Easter occurred together with the discovery of the empty tomb and are therefore naturally more interested in the miraculous aspect of the event. And by presenting the event in this way they give an obvious indication of having a shortened historical perspective. The discovery of the empty tomb, which in my opinion—and here I agree with H. von Campenhausen—could have marked the beginning of the Easter-event, and the first dawning of what it meant, are compressed into one scene in both Mark and Matthew (the latter being dependent upon Mark). In addition to their apologetic and missionary interests Luke and John aim at presenting the historical truth. This means therefore that their description of the sequence of events is much more complicated.[27] John describes separately and in detail, for example, the discovery of the empty tomb by the women, then the first dawning of the Easter faith of the disciples who ran to the grave, then Mary Magdalene's full understanding of the meaning of Easter and then finally an appearance to all the disciples. Luke and John, in contrast to Mark and Matthew, lay stronger emphasis on the fact that the main events took place in Jerusalem. Thus by clarifying the sequence of events in this way they deliberately limit themselves to the original event alone.

2. *Isolating and Securing the Original Event.*

By limiting the tradition in this way to the original event on Easter Sunday the question as to whom Jesus first appeared inevitably arose: was it to the women, who according to most of the Gospel accounts were the first to find out about the empty tomb? or was it to the disciples? If we are right in suggesting that the leading intention was to clarify and sort out the beginnings of the Easter-event, then this question about priority was bound to crop up. The way in which the Gospels handle this question shows that the tradition about the discovery of the empty tomb by the women was judged to be of considerable historical importance.

It is quite striking that when there is no report of an appearance of Christ to the women (or to Mary Magdalene) then there is always a report of an appearance to Peter. On the other hand, when there is any indication of an appearance to Peter, there is either no reference at all to an appearance to the women or such an appearance is flatly denied. Thus perhaps we can say that reports of an appearance of Christ to the women are always lacking whenever a specific Petrine influence seems to be the determining factor in the Gospel account.

It is reasonably clear that Mark's Gospel (apart from the ending which was added later), points to a future revelatory event which will involve 'Peter and the disciples', (Mark 16 : 7). There is no account of an appearance of Christ to the women. Matthew does give an account of an appearance to the women, but at the same time the rôle played by Peter in the sequence of events becomes secondary, (Matt. 28 : 7). Luke speaks about a first appearance of Christ to Peter (in a surprisingly casual way), but makes no mention of any appearance to the women and in fact denies such an appearance, (Luke 24 : 34; 24 : 24). John gives no account of any appearance to Peter but emphasises all the more the fact that Jesus first revealed himself to Mary Magdalene. The sequence in the ending of Mark, which was added later, refers specifically to this appearance as being the 'first'. This gives a clear indication of the intentions of those who wrote this ending, (Mark 16 : 9). By this time the tradition concerning the appearance to Peter must have been generally known and accepted. But by omitting any reference to this appearance, the later ending of Mark shows how much the writers' interest was focussed on the question of the one to whom Jesus first appeared, for the first appearance would be regarded as the most decisive. In this context names were of no particular importance. These recognisable lines of the development of the traditions make it likely—and here we point to the following conclusion—that because of this one-sided interest in the first and most decisive appearance, other stable traditions could be omitted. It is obvious that the tradition concerning the appearance of Jesus to Peter belongs to this category. If we examine the tradition about the first appearance we can recognise that the Evangelists were much more interested in the first appearance of Christ as such than in the person to whom he first appeared. The truth of this event is impressed upon the reader, but the way in which the Evangelists select certain aspects of the event and the various means of illustration which they use should not be judged according to modern historical criteria.

The possibility that certain special Petrine traditions have influenced some of the Gospel accounts can be seen from the fact that Mark suggests an appearance of Christ to Peter and Luke actually testifies to one. This is supported by the point of view expressed in the appendix to the Fourth Gospel, (i.e., chapter 21, which is not Johannine), which deals with the first call of Peter, and also by the account in the apocryphal Gospel of Peter which is also of some importance. The Gospel of Peter describes how the women have a vision of a young man at the graveside (following the Markan account), and reports that the risen Christ first appeared to Peter in Galilee, (v. 55-60). This also corresponds to the rule which was outlined at the beginning of this section.

The fact that all the Gospels and Paul give an account of the appearance to the Eleven, or at least hint at such an appearance, (as with Mark), can be taken as a proof of the historical stability of the tradition.[28] At the same time this provides a useful insight into the theological significance of this tradition which has always been accepted and retained. It was important to point out which appearance came first, whether to the women or to Peter, in order to emphasise the truth of the sequence of events. At first only a few people were involved in this sequence, then soon after, all the disciples. It is quite likely that from the very beginning the appearance of Jesus to the Eleven was generally regarded as the ground for calling anew the representatives of the people of God, who had already gathered before Easter, and as the basis of the obligation to mission, (Matt. 19 : 28; Luke 22 : 30). This is supported by the fact that even those Gospels which extend the period of the Easter-event beyond this appearance to the Eleven, (see John 20 : 24ff.; Luke 24 : 50ff.), nevertheless do not connect the commissioning of the disciples to the farewell-scene where it would most naturally belong.

The story of the disciples on the road to Emmaus is the only one which has survived from an originally vast number of Easter traditions.[29] At first sight this looks like an exception to the principle of selection which was mentioned above, because it deals neither with the first appearance nor with the decisive event in the experience of the first disciples. But it may in fact act as a confirmation of this principle, because from the very beginning this story was always handed down as one dealing with events which were closely related in time to the event on Easter Sunday and (in addition!) it had the advantage of containing the testimony of some relatives of the Lord. This story then, which appears to be an exception to the rule, actually provides a very good proof that the process of reduction and selection behind the Easter tradition remained basically determined by the intention to impress and to secure the truth of Easter Sunday. What Paul aimed at in I Cor. 15 with his long list of witnesses, corresponds exactly to what the Gospels do when they strictly limit and select. Towards the end of the century what mattered was not the many witnesses, for this would probably have raised more problems than it solved, (see 1 Cor. 9 : 1).[30] What really mattered were the few definite and trustworthy reports. The history of the Easter traditions can be properly understood only when we take into account the fact that they had to retain the basic and final truth through many chances and changes: the truth that the Lord is risen indeed.

3. *The necessary Interpretation of the Empty Tomb.*

Among the material which has been handed down the story of the empty tomb is of considerable importance. What sort of rôle does this play in the Easter-event, and what possible consequences may it have for the question about the discipleship which originated in that event? It is commonly held that the story of the empty tomb, which has the literary form of a legend, acted as a proof of the resurrection for the early writers.[31] It is said that it was developed exactly for this particular purpose. But this is a view which cannot be sustained, for it is not difficult to show that the 'empty tomb' was never regarded as a sufficient means for interpreting the Easter-event, but from the very beginning was understood to be something which itself required interpretation. This provides fairly secure grounds for holding that we are not dealing with a later legend but with a historical detail of some considerable importance. It could never be simply relied upon as a safe argument for the truth. It was much more necessary to come to some understanding of it, just as its adversaries had to do, (Matt. 28 : 12).

According to the way in which it has been edited and according to its subject-matter, the main features of the story show that it belongs to the self-contained passion-narrative complex which, as is well known, gives a very careful description of the burial of Jesus, (see Mark 15 : 42ff.; par. John 19 : 38ff.). If the passion-narrative contains the oldest closed unit of traditional material then the story of the empty tomb cannot be excluded from it. For internal reasons the story is in fact more than probable. For closest relatives it was a religious duty to mourn the dead. In this respect the first three days of mourning were of special importance.[32] It should also be noted that the more historical versions of Luke and John are strikingly similar. Both of them report that the disciples ran to the grave. Luke 24 : 12, which is unquestionably original,[33] and John 20 : 4f. are similar even as regards formulation, and it is most likely that the latter amounts to a rather remarkable correction of the Lukan account.[34] The brief report which tells how Peter ran to the tomb, stooped, looked in and saw the cloths, has been corrected[35] by the writer of the Fourth Gospel to show that the 'other disciple' also ran to the tomb with Peter and not Peter alone. According to the Fourth Gospel it was the disciple John who stooped down and who was the first to see the cloths, although Peter was the first to go into the tomb. The brief report in Luke also mentions the fact that a number of disciples ran to the tomb, (24 : 22ff.). We are told that the women had 'a vision of angels' at the graveside. After this, some of the disciples are said to have gone to the grave. Even if our judgement about the historical value of the details of these descriptions has to be a cautious one we may nevertheless accept that they are historically more probable than the assumption that the disciples immediately fled to Galilee, (for which the necessary sources are lacking).[36]

Can any conclusion be drawn from this with regard to Easter discipleship? Was the empty tomb a proof of the Easter faith, or was it even perhaps that which itself gave rise to the Easter faith of the disciples? Here it has to be emphasised that with both the early and the later community the empty tomb was never in any way regarded as being a sufficient ground for the truth of the Easter faith. The discovery of the empty tomb was always reported as an important part of the sequence of events, but was never itself taken as proof for God's action.

It should be pointed out that none of the Gospel stories dealing with this theme make any mention of an appearance of Christ which is directly connected with the empty tomb, as we would normally expect. Even Matthew, who gives a very detailed description of the opening of the tomb by an angel who has descended from heaven, says nothing about Christ leaving the tomb. The angel simply answers the question about where the risen Christ is to be found. Here the Evangelist appears to be somewhat illogical, for we actually expect that the living Christ will now appear. Luke emphasises the perplexity of the disciples and their obstinate lack of faith when confronted by the empty tomb. We can by no means assume from the Lukan account that the Easter faith was spontaneously evoked in the disciples when faced with the empty tomb. It is rather the case that the Easter faith always arises in the experience of an encounter with the risen Christ. In John's Gospel, for instance, the disciples themselves consider the possibility that the body may have been secretly removed, (John 20 : 2. 13). The theory that the grave was robbed does not necessarily have to be traced back to the Jews alone, (Matt. 28 : 13-15). It may rather indicate the doubts of the disciples and of the followers of Jesus themselves. From a human point of view it is much more likely that they thought that the body of Jesus had been taken away by the Romans in order to prevent his followers from later honouring and worshipping him. If this interpretation is correct then the historical fact of the discovery of the empty tomb by the disciples is not something which relieves them of their doubt, but is actually the cause of their doubt. This is just as much the case today as it was then. The history of the tradition even allows for the uncertainty of the disciples as far as the empty tomb is concerned. Whenever there is any tendency to make use of the 'empty tomb' in itself as a kind of proof for the resurrection, such a procedure eventually leads nowhere because even further proofs have to be added, (cf. the references to the guard at the graveside, Matt. 27 : 66; or to the linen cloths and napkin, Luke 24 : 12; John 20 : 6f.). The ground and origin of the Easter faith of the disciples was never merely an object or objects such as this.

It always consisted in a personal encounter with the living Christ and his Word. Nevertheless, in our view, the empty tomb is a more important and more legitimate factor in what we must take to be the historical sequence of events. This then is the situation. The *angelus interpres* (Mark 16 : 5) was required, because the empty tomb could never act as its own interpreter in any satisfactory way.

4. *The dialectical Relationship between the Cross and Easter.*

A closer examination of the Easter traditions leads one to the conclusion that the theme of the 'end-time' (in the eschatological-apocalyptic sense) was not something which first became significant because of the Easter-event. If our interpretation is correct, then this idea was already present from the beginning of the sequence of events, nor can we rule out the possibility that it was already present even prior to Easter. The apocalyptic interpretation of the Christ-event which began with Easter was in all probability not based upon belief in the resurrection of Jesus alone. There are good grounds for assuming that it existed already prior to the Easter faith of the disciples and even prior to Good Friday. Nor should it be forgotten that Jesus' proclamation of the coming reign of God resulted in his death. According to the unanimous conviction of the early community the temporal point which marked the advent of God's new reality was the death of Jesus. A number of recent studies allow for this interpretation and take the view that the resurrection was probably at first regarded as the first act of Jesus' expected return.[37]

It is quite true that to a large extent New Testament research still tends to deal with the Easter stories in isolation. H. Grass and H. von Campenhausen do not take sufficient account of the eschatological dimension in the historical event of Easter *and* the cross. They deal with the Easter reports of the Gospels as isolated units and do not consider the possibility of approaching the problem in the light of the highly eschatological frame of reference, an element which is historically well attested, which forms the background to Jesus' proclamation and which is the key to his Person. However meticulous their approach, they have been unable to grasp the events concerning Jesus as a whole and as a unity.

There is also the widespread opinion that as the sayings of Jesus have been handed down they have been more and more apocalypticised. This may be true to a certain extent. But the rule is not applicable where the Easter tradition is concerned.[38] In fact the situation is quite the reverse. The history of the Easter tradition is not one which has been increasingly apocalypticised. It rather shows evidence of an increasing de-apocalypticising. Apocalyptic is there at the beginning of the sequence of events; that is to say, there existed the certainty among the followers of Jesus, even when confronted with the incomprehensible fact of his death, that God would reveal himself.

Paul, who is the first to hand down a list of witnesses, takes the view that the end of the Aeon has already come, (1 Cor. 10 : 11). He is convinced that 'the day is at hand' (Rom. 13 : 11ff.). He dates the new age from the death of Christ, for example with the words: 'the old has passed away, behold, the new has come', (2 Cor. 5 : 17ff.). Paul dates the exaltation of Jesus from the cross, (Phil. 2 : 5ff.), which makes it coincide with the beginning of the new eschatological age. From this point, to live as a disciple necessarily means living 'between the times'. It is in this situation that the 'Word of the Cross' is proclaimed, believed and appropriated, (1 Cor. 1 : 18ff.). Because of Jesus' obedience this is the Word which guarantees God's presence and his suffering with the world. Therefore the new Aeon is decisively the Aeon of God's salvation, grace and righteousness. The advent of the new takes place in a confrontation with the cross and the relation of the old and finished Aeon to the end is made clear, (Gal. 3 : 23ff.). Paul obviously points to the ultimate mystery of the Christian message when he says that the 'Word of the Cross' is a 'Word of power'.

Like Paul, the first Evangelist also regards the cross of Jesus as the point at which the eschatological Aeon has broken in and as the point from which he dates a new divine reality.[39] For Mark the cross is identical with 'the hour of the Son of Man', (Mark 14 : 41). The death of Jesus is intentionally described in very close connection with the Old Testament idea of God's Last Day, (cf. Mark; 15 : 33ff., and Amos 8 : 9 LXX). While Mark still retains an unqualified eschatological understanding of the suffering and death of Jesus, this is no longer the case with Matthew and Luke. In these Gospels the eschatological interpretation gives way to an understanding of salvation which is strongly influenced by the idea that the time of the Messiah has begun. Both of these writers reckon with the last days which are still to come, (Matt. 1 : 1ff.; Luke 3 : 23ff.), and Luke in particular presents the Jewish Messianology in a way which shows strong Hellenistic influences. Nevertheless, by sifting the traditional material with which they have worked, there are sufficient grounds for concluding that this was based upon an older eschatological interpretation of the life and death of Jesus which has later been modified. This is also one of the striking things about John's Gospel. John has reduced the futuristic eschatology to a minimum, but steadfastly insists that Jesus' death signifies the eschatological hour in which salvation is wholly fulfilled, (John 19 : 30). John states clearly that the raising of the cross is simultaneously the glorification of Jesus and the anticipated *krisis* (judgement) of the world,[40] (John 12 : 31f.). Clearly the original apocalyptic terminology is given a new validity, but in contrast to apocalyptic as such its content is quite new. It appears therefore that what we call the Easter-event is the insoluble compound of the events of Good Friday and of Easter.

The concept of the Easter-event has recently been questioned by W. Marxsen.[41] His view is that we can only speak of Easter as something which *happened* to the disciples. According to Marxsen, this 'happening' was not the resurrection as such, but the fact that Jesus was *seen* by the disciples. Easter as an 'event' is said to be something beyond our historical experience. This view is correct in the sense that it is impossible to substantiate the Easter-event historically as the basis of post-Easter discipleship, and if the 'event' is limited one-sidedly to the 'resurrection of Jesus' alone. The Easter-event is something which can be grasped by us only in the Easter-faith with its world- and life-changing power, and through the re-gathering of the disciples who recognised their duty to witness, to preach and to carry out their missionary task, thus putting their faith into practice. This being the case, the question of the *event* becomes extremely acute, especially in view of the fact that the disciples began their task anew as confronted by the death of Jesus, the event which marks the catastrophic conclusion to his earthly life and ministry. Faced with the death of Jesus, from the very start the disciples were thus also faced with the fundamental question as to whether God had confirmed or rejected Jesus. This means that the real problem is not so much whether Jesus was raised, but whether God was present in the death of Jesus as the living God.[42] The problem of the event is thus raised primarily by the death of Jesus and not by his resurrection. The death of Jesus therefore poses the question whether God confirms the obedience of faith or not.[43]

If the resurrection is treated as an isolated possibility then the question becomes much too academic. No one who believes in God would deny that it is possible for him to raise the dead. The more important question is rather whether God fully confirms a life which was marked by complete self-giving and by total obedience. If God was present in the exemplary obedience of the suffering and dying Jesus, whose life was committed to God even in the situation of absolute God-forsakenness, then God is also the living God who shows himself victorious in these events. According to the early Christian witness it was because of his obedience that Jesus was exalted, (Phil. 2 : 5ff.), and so became the model for the faith of his disciples.

The dialectical relationship between the death *and* the resurrection of Jesus, in which, because of Jesus' obedience, God revealed himself as God *for* us, signified for the earliest disciples the supreme moment of eschatological revelation, and consequently this was declared to be identical with the coming of the 'turn of the ages'.

5. *Avoiding the Extremes of Gnosticism and of Apocalypticism.*

From the previous section it can be seen that Easter was bound up with the re-emergence of eschatological hopes. In the early Christian tradition the resurrection of Jesus is treated in terms of apocalyptic. This meant that the expectation of the end necessarily again came to the fore. The pre-Easter hope which was contained in the proclamation and in the ministry of Jesus was revived and believers reckoned with the possibility of experiencing an appearance of the exalted Christ from heaven. This expectation most probably sprang up immediately and spontaneously with Easter. It was not something which gradually developed along with the growing Easter-faith. In such a situation there was the danger that the eschatological hope would be interpreted in a one-sidedly apocalyptic way. This danger was at first very great. But in fact it was avoided and we can see that the later teaching and witness were characterised by a remarkable present-future interpretation of the Christ-event.[44] This meant the certainty that the risen One was not only present, but would also be present in the future. And since it viewed the event in this way, the earliest community understood salvation in terms of a tension between present and future. However, there was another danger. The longer they lived in this world the more they would be tempted to give up their expectation of the future. The conviction that in a certain sense Jesus was spiritually present might have led believers to sublimate the tension of their faith, to which the future expectation was fundamental, either by means of speculation or by taking a mystical view of the revelation. However, the history of the Easter tradition shows that this danger of interpreting the event in a Gnostic fashion was a danger of which they were aware and which they managed consciously to avoid. This point can be illustrated with reference to the so-called 'Galilee-saying'. The texts are as follows:

(a) Mark 14 : 28, where Jesus says; 'But after I am raised up, I will go before you to Galilee'. Matt. 26 : 32 is an exact parallel to this.

(b) Mark 16 : 7: 'He is going before you to Galilee; there you will see him, as he told you' (the words of the young man at the tomb). Shortly after this the narrative breaks off.

(c) Matt. 28 : 7: 'He has risen from the dead, and behold, he is going before you to Galilee; there you will see him. Lo, I have told you' (the angel to the women at the tomb). This text could be a conflation of Mark 14 : 28 and Mark 16 : 7.

(d) Matt. 28 : 10: 'Go and tell my brethren to go to Galilee, and there they will see me' (the words of the risen Christ). Here Matthew clarifies his own position.

(e) Luke 24 : 6f.: 'Remember how he told you, while he was still in Galilee, that the Son of Man must be delivered into the hands of sinful men, and be crucified, and on the third day rise' (the two angels at the tomb).

(f) Luke 24 : 50: 'Then he led them out as far as Bethany, and lifting up his hands he blessed them . . . (and) parted from them.' Luke takes the view that the risen Christ accompanied the disciples 'in the body', if not to Galilee then certainly towards Bethany.

(g) John 20 : 17: 'Go to my brethren and say to them: "I am ascending to my Father and to your Father, to my God and your God"' (Jesus' words to Mary Magdalene. John presents a later development of the Matt. 28 : 10 tradition).

(h) The Gospel of Peter, 56: 'He is risen and has gone away. . . . He is risen and has gone to the place from which he was sent' (the young man at the tomb). This is followed by a hint that the disciples returned to Galilee where it was likely that a revelation would take place. The words, 'the place from which he was sent' may therefore be meant either literally or symbolically.

(i) The Gnostic Apocryphon of John[45]: 'He (a pharisee) said to him (John): "He has returned from whence he came"'. Notice the close correspondence to (h) and therefore also to (g).

(j) Gnostic Wisdom of Jesus Christ[46]: 'After he had risen from the dead there came up to Galilee and on to the mountain his twelve disciples and seven women who had followed him as disciples . . . and the Saviour appeared to them, not in his original form but as an invisible spirit.' Hereafter follow Gnostic disclosures.

Texts (a) to (f) demonstrate the way in which the saying has been altered within the so-called canonical tradition. Text (h) comes from an apocryphal Jewish-Christian Gospel which may contain certain Gnostic influences. These facts are in themselves remarkable enough. Thus we have sufficient grounds for having dealt with them quite briefly.

Mark, the earliest of the Gospel-writers, quotes a traditional saying concerning the reunion of the disciples under the Master who goes before them and who in the meantime has been established as the eschatological Lord, (cf. Mark 14 : 27). This gives the impression of being an enlarged Master-disciple concept, an image magnified to transcendent proportions. If this is the case, then the disciples would have expected that he whom God had confirmed as Messiah, Son of Man and Shepherd, would gather his followers in this new time of revelation and lead them to the promised goal.[47] However, it is still questionable whether this definitely pre-Easter hope had always been linked with 'the promised land' of Galilee.[48] It is possible, for example, that Mark, who was writing at the time of the Jewish-Roman War (cf. the flight to Pella), related this expectation with a specific place.[49] It certainly looks as though part of Mark 14 : 28 has been given a post-Easter form. Mark 16 : 7 then may be understood to refer only to a 'going before' in the purely temporal sense and not, as it had originally been understood, namely, as a 'going together' with the Master and under his guidance. The 'seeing' in Mark 16 : 7, as in the original version, probably means to 'behold' Jesus enthroned as the Messiah and Son of Man, (cf. Mark 14 : 62 and Ps. 110 : 1 and Dan. 7 : 13).[50] The possibility that the later lost ending of this Gospel may already have changed the content of this hope cannot be ruled out. From the perspective of the later community it may be the case that it was no longer found acceptable. The present ending of the Gospel shows that the journey to Galilee was not the result of the report of the women, (Mark 16 : 8 emphasises their silence), but rather was occasioned by an event in which Christ revealed himself directly to 'Peter and the disciples', (see Mark 16 : 7). Even the oldest Markan version seems to have referred to an important appearance of Christ in Jerusalem which involved Peter and the disciples. Matthew and Luke, both of whom probably knew the original ending, altered it, each in his own way. Matthew connects the 'seeing' with the final and most important appearance, (see Matt. 28 : 17). By having the risen Christ repeat the Galilee-saying. the misleading 'going before them' (which here is meant first in the local sense, secondly in the temporal) is finally resolved. Consequently, Matt. 28 : 10 has to be understood as simply pointing to the fact that the disciples should 'set out' (for Galilee) on their own. The fact should not be overlooked that in the account of this final appearance there is a clear echo of Dan. 7 : 13. This appearance which was initially understood as final and as eschatological has now become the appearance of Christ which points forward to the future.[51]

Although in Luke there is a formal hint about a Galilean location, he has given up the Galilee-saying completely because with time it had become more difficult to understand. Instead of the eschatological mystery which began with Easter, Luke speaks about the mystery of Jesus' suffering.[52] We must also notice that in addition to this he also describes the journey of the risen One together with the disciples to Bethany (although this takes place after the main appearance). This is important because it may well reflect the original Markan tradition of a journey together to Galilee, a tradition which, in our opinion, was still known to his (Luke's) other two sources. Both Matthew and Luke drew up their accounts, each handling his source in his own individual way. Matthew, who seeks to avoid the idea that Jesus accompanied the disciples 'in the body', holds fast to Galilee as the place of the appearance. Luke, who places the event in Jerusalem, retains the idea that the risen One accompanied the disciples (see also Luke 24 : 13ff.). Nevertheless he has given up the idea that the disciples went all together to *Galilee*. It is also worth noting that Luke gives particular emphasis to the complex eschatological question, a question which is said to have been answered by the risen One in principle, (Acts 1 : 3b; 6f.).

John sets out to convey an even deeper understanding of the saying and in 20 : 16ff. he includes the tradition of Matt. 28 : 9f., and reshapes it, (cf. the typical phrase 'my brethren').[53] The idea of a Galilean 'promised land' seems to have been completely set aside, along with the notion of a miraculous and at the same time realistic journey together, whether over a larger or a shorter distance. John stresses that heaven is the place of promise from which the (pre-existent) Lord has come and to which he has returned again so that his disciples might also be with him there, (John 16 : 16, 22 etc.). The saying is phrased in such a way as to express the ultimate, not the penultimate truth of the Easter-event. It is even possible that

66

this compares most closely with the pre-Easter content of this saying. If this interpretation is correct then Jesus' hope was that the people of God would be gathered together in a realm beyond history.[54]

The early history of the Galilean-saying indicates the danger which existed of an apocalyptic misinterpretation of the Easter-event. The fact that this kind of interpretation was at their immediate disposal meant that the disciples probably found themselves faced with a critical situation. On the other hand, the later history of the tradition shows that there was the possibility of an increasingly Gnostic tendency to speculate which thus threatened to obscure it. The clear message of Easter was no longer taken seriously but became a means to an end, a means of conveying mysteries and revelations. In the Gospel of Peter this tendency is not yet fully developed even though this document is characterised by a certain preference for imaginative speculation. As with John (20 : 17) the Galilee-saying is here no longer a problem. The sentence: 'He is risen and has gone to the place from which he was sent' in the context could still possibly refer to Galilee, but it is more likely that this has a symbolic meaning, as is the case with John 20 : 17.

Concerning the last two Gnostic texts however, the situation is quite clear. Here the religious interest centres upon the question as to where the Saviour had come from and what secret revelations he had brought into the world. Therefore we can appreciate the achievement of the Evangelists when we consider that by a process of reduction and selection of the tradition, and in spite of the fact that they were faced with a very complex situation, they put an end to this falsifying tendency. Thus it is not surprising that John's Gospel marks the end of the canonical Gospel tradition.

In summing up we may say that the Galilee-saying tradition clearly occupied a position between two extremes, both of which had to be resisted: apocalyptic materialism and Gnostic spiritualisation. Both of these were dangerous to the Easter message. However, the outcome was successful in the sense that both the present soteriological significance of the Easter-event and its eschatological-future significance were retained.

6. *What Factors marked the Beginning of the Tradition?*

Judging by the history of the Easter tradition it is quite clear that it did not originate in a vacuum. What marks the beginning of this tradition is neither poetic imagination nor religious enthusiasm. And although there are a variety of accounts this does not in any way count against the subjective truth of the testimony. The chief aim of all the writers is to clarify and mark the outlines of the actual event. Its ground is the certainty and the experience that the Crucified lives. Since that Easter Sunday the Easter faith is present in the world as a power which has shaped the outlook and the endeavours of all disciples. What is the basis of this faith? Evidently it is in the experiences of the women and of the disciples who regarded their knowledge of the Easter-event as being something beyond dispute. It concerned first of all the women, then Peter and finally the rest of the disciples. The details can no longer be exactly established because the Gospel-reports which have come down to us do not lend themselves to precise scientific-historical examination. But each in his own way, and using different means of expression, hold fast to the one truth: the Lord is risen. The accompanying external considerations which are open to change and to re-shaping almost always act as illustrations of this testimony. It is quite clear that the different accounts have been formed in accordance with certain rules of development. There can be no doubt that the beginning of the tradition is marked by the overwhelming recognition of the deeply eschatological significance of the event. It is likely that the question of a bodily resurrection was not at first of any great importance.[55] It is rather the case that the pre-Easter expectations were revived. But these expectations are now based upon the full knowledge that the Crucified has been confirmed by God and 'exalted' because of his obedience.[56]

The powerful effects of this first Easter faith were immediately felt far and wide. The pre-Easter disciples (probably on the initiative of Peter) were firmly reunited once again. Other groups were also attracted and convinced. The subjective sharing of the experience must at first have played a quite considerable rôle, although the objective nature of *what* had been seen was never itself a matter of dispute. At first the hopes of the disciples were probably directed towards the immediate eschatological appearance in Galilee of the One whom they had seen risen. We know nothing in detail about the experiences of the disciples in Galilee. However, the eschatological expectation was certainly not fulfilled. The experience of the risen One (in whatever sense this was understood, e.g. as present in the Word or in the Spirit), served to deepen the certainty that God would complete that process which he had already initiated before Easter and gather his people under the sign of the cross. And Jesus' Easter disciples themselves knew that by dedication and obedience they also would be led toward that new reality into which their Lord had already been taken up. There can be no doubt that in the event of the cross the first disciples recognised the beginning of the 'kingdom of God' and that in the Word of the cross they saw its continuing and victorious realisation. The resurrection of Jesus was never of any significance as such. It was rather the background to the witness that the Crucified was alive, and that his obedience unto death is the key to the mystery of God's decisive action.[57]

III. *Discipleship in the Light of the Patterns of the Easter-event*

(1) Each Evangelist gives his own account of the Easter-event, and the disciples appear in a different light according to where the emphasis is placed in the individual reports. *Mark's* Gospel, in the shortened form in which it has come down to us, gives no account of the resurrection. We are told only about the journey of the women to the tomb and their perplexity and fear when confronted by the miracle which had taken place. The Evangelist apparently reckons with a group of disciples who at first found themselves without a leader and quite unable to come to any decision; a group, who came to realise the truth, not through the reports of the women, but by means of an experience of their own which was of the utmost importance to them. The idea that the disciples would re-assemble in the eschatological hour was obviously of special

importance to Mark. And for him, discipleship is a discipleship under the eschatological sign of the cross, which is itself the sign of the mystery of the suffering of the Son of Man.[58]

By contrast, *Matthew*, in the closing chapters of the Gospel, gives a description of an almost timeless revelation of the risen One to the disciples. The risen Christ delegates his authority to the Eleven, issues his command to mission, and to baptise, and promises his disciples that he will be with them always. It is his will that all nations should be his disciples. They should also do what Jesus, the earthly Master, had taught his disciples. The risen One does not appear before his disciples in a spectacular epiphany as one might expect. Rather it is as 'Lord of the World' and as One who in principle is already known to the Christian community, that he addresses them. The discipleship which is consequent upon Easter is primarily a commitment to follow the Word of Jesus, the Messiah.[59]

Luke describes how the disciples are introduced to the mystery of his suffering and resurrection by the living Lord himself. On several occasions he makes reference to the mystery of salvation, (Luke 24 : 7; 24 : 26ff.; 24 : 32; 24 : 44ff.), a mystery which can be disclosed through searching the scriptures. From this awareness of the salvation-event, which according to the third Evangelist had been planned from the very beginning, there is developed a new understanding of history, a history in which discipleship must now be lived. The promise to the disciples is firmly bound to history, (cf. Luke 24 : 49; Acts 1 : 4), and is addressed to a community which is certain of the world-changing presence of its Lord in Word and Sacrament.[60]

John describes Easter-discipleship as a relationship based upon new knowledge and upon a new revelation. The disciples come to know the risen One in hearing his voice, (20 : 14ff., cf. 10 : 4). At the same time they share in a new relationship to one another, the mark of which is God's revelation of himself as Father. The leading concept of this Evangelist is very much determined by the idea of the unity between Master and disciples, a unity based upon knowing, believing and witnessing. The disciples enter a new reality. They are not left in mourning and in fear by their departing Lord, but are

70

commissioned as messengers of the truth, of peace, joy and forgiveness, (20 : 20ff.).[61]

(2) Although we have these individual descriptions of discipleship in the light of the Easter-event, the fact of the unity behind this witness must not be overlooked. For this reason we may now go on to point out some of those aspects which determine the character of Christian discipleship from Easter onwards.

1. *Discipleship and the Tension between Doubt and Certainty.*

If Christian discipleship simply meant following in the light of Easter then clearly it would be characterised by certainty alone. However, since this discipleship became a reality only in connection with the dialectical relationship between the cross and Easter, it is also a discipleship which is characterised by uncertainty and by the temptation to doubt. The remarks of the first disciples already provide evidence of what was probably their immediate reaction: 'They have taken the Lord away'. Even the appearances of the Lord to Peter and the disciples, about which we can be fairly certain, did not result in immediate certainty. The way in which the Evangelists describe the reactions of the disciples is extremely varied. We are told about their fear, (Mark 16 : 16), their fear and trembling, (Mark 16 : 8), their helplessness and their perplexity, (Luke 24 : 4). Their response to the news is even marked by mockery and unbelief, (Luke 24 : 11). Nowhere is it stated that their reaction to what had happened and to what was said was one of immediate certainty. Even Matthew, who clothes his account very much in terms of the miraculous, stresses that the women were overcome with 'fear and joy', (Matt. 28 : 8). Even in the report of the final Galilean appearance the reaction of the disciples is one of doubt, (Matt. 28 : 17). Luke notes that at first, for joy and astonishment, the disciples could not believe, (Luke 24 : 41). In the story of the journey to Emmaus the disciples become fully certain only after the risen One has vanished, (Luke 24 : 31f.). In the later ending of Mark, the risen One upbraids his disciples for their unbelief, (Mark 16 : 14). All this first of all expresses the one motif which runs through all the reports, namely, the awe of the disciples when confronted by the revelatory events. In addition to this however, we also have to ask whether behind this there may be a legitimate theological and historical intention. As regards the first point it can be said that the experience of the disciples was certainly subjective.[62] The reaction of doubt was quite natural because of the nature of the events themselves. Nevertheless, since the victorious Easter-faith and the determination and decisiveness of the disciples are historical fact, we may conclude that the event itself was of an elementally powerful nature. The theological intention underlying the reports is most clearly expressed by John. He links the first awakening of the Easter-faith not with an appearance but with the discovery of the empty tomb. We are told in chapter 20 : 8 that the disciple who ran with Peter to the tomb and who was the first to reach it, came to believe in the risen One when confronted by the empty grave. This of course should not be taken to mean that the empty tomb must be understood as a guarantee of the resurrection faith.[63] Rather, chapter 20 : 9, and the context in which it is placed, show that this faith should be understood as an example, as the model of that faith which breaks through to the truth out of the open and doubtful situation. The story of Thomas expresses this intention most clearly. The true greatness of the faith of the disciples is that it is not based on sight, (20 : 29). And that which is generally called the Easter-event was never simply unambiguous, it is equally an event which can arouse unbelief. Even the first disciples could not avoid the basic decision of faith. And it is quite clear that from the beginning they found themselves placed within this special reality of faith, in the tension between certainty and doubt in which faith comes into its own and is strengthened.[64] This really means that the disciples' temptation to doubt should not be judged as a failure. It points rather to the actual sphere in which discipleship is accepted, in which it develops to its fullest extent and in which it finds its true vocation. Thomas's doubt is not uncharacteristic of discipleship. It is an attitude which is characteristic of the conduct of any disciple. With regard to our own situation it might be asked whether one should expect more from the people of our own time than that which the disciples themselves were able to achieve in their encounter with the living One.

2. Since Easter, Discipleship is lived under the promise of suffering and of life.

The words of the earthly Lord concerning discipleship were deepened and given a more radical interpretation in the post-Easter period in the sense that they now constitute a call to share the destiny of the crucified and risen Lord. To live with Jesus now means to suffer with him and even to die with him. The pre-Easter call to share one's life and destiny with the Master is now seen against the background of the powerful example of Jesus' own destiny and is thus seen in a more radical light.[65] It is true that until Easter the denial of self and suffering together with the Master were considered only as possibilities; from Easter on however, these are the true marks of discipleship: 'If we have died with him, we shall also live with him,' (2 Tim. 2 : 11). The life of Paul shows that this almost proverbial saying is not one which is to be understood only in a figurative sense. Living and suffering, understood as self-denial, responsibility, persecution, signify in Paul's case the actual experience of the missionary.[66] He always carries the death of Jesus in the body, so that the life of Jesus may also be manifested in it, (2 Cor. 4 : 10). The reality in which he lives is that reality which has come into the world in the One who was crucified and is risen. Nor are these ideas confined to Paul alone.

Generally speaking, the pre-Easter sayings became clearer and more meaningful in the light of the truth enshrined in Jesus' destiny. Although the idea of the suffering of the just man was a leading theme in late Judaism and a theme which is incorporated in the message of Jesus as well, the post-Easter material is nevertheless of a much more specific character. It is founded upon Jesus' historical Word and re-presents the destiny of Jesus with a new actuality. Paul, for example, gives the instruction that everyone should have that mind which was in Christ Jesus, (Phil. 2 : 5). The example which he holds up is Jesus' voluntary and obedient humiliation unto death, even the death of the cross. The re-formulation of the sayings concerning discipleship into sayings about bearing and taking up the cross are also to be seen in this light.[67] These sayings were most probably written down after the time of Paul; but it

73

is fairly clear that these re-formulations noted above were derived from the same early Christian theology of the Word *and* destiny of Jesus, just as this theology was later developed by Paul in his own individual way. The disciple is not greater than his Lord. This now applies chiefly to the question of living and suffering together, (Matt. 10 : 24 and context; Luke 6 : 40; John 13 : 16; 15 : 20). Whenever the disciple regards this possibility as an unreasonable demand upon him, he is not on the side of God but of Satan, (Mark 8 : 33). This text is found in the Gospel of Mark in the episode where Peter is reprimanded by Jesus who has just made intimation of his readiness to suffer. Sayings concerning the inevitable suffering of the disciples are quite intentionally placed at the close of this episode. The first saying demands self-denial and that one should take up the cross. The metaphor about bearing the cross is probably meant to underline the idea of necessary renunciation which is the meaning of discipleship, (Mark 8 : 34ff.). What is considered here is the possibility that one may have to give oneself even unto death. The saying is conditional, (so also the parallel sayings, Matt. 16 : 24; Luke 9 : 23), but seems to imply that if one is to be a disciple then one must inevitably be prepared to suffer. The saying which follows is given in a repetitive form: 'For whoever would save his life will lose it, and whoever loses his life for my sake and the Gospel's will save it'. The phrase 'and the Gospel's' is a post-Easter re-formulation. This indicates therefore that this saying of Jesus was once again made binding by the early church in its missionary situation. The Markan saying about bearing the cross (with its hint of martyrdom) is similarly altered by Luke when he speaks about taking up one's cross 'daily', (Luke 9 : 23). His intention is to point out that discipleship is to be realised in the normal situations of daily life and not only in exceptional situations. Discipleship can indeed mean the daily readiness to deny oneself. The double saying in Mark 8 : 34ff. appears again in an altered form in Matt. 10 : 38f. and in Luke 14 : 27 and 17 : 33. It is most likely that these altered forms are derived from the sayings-source. These differing re-formulations are again very revealing. Matthew says that he who does not take up his cross and follow is not worthy of Jesus. This is apparently aimed at Christians who should not forget what they have already received. Luke however, says that whoever does not bear 'his own' cross and follow cannot be 'my', i.e. Jesus', disciple. It is quite probable that speaking out of the missionary situation, Luke is trying to point out what one has to be prepared for if he wishes to become a disciple. In this way there is a remarkably intimate connection in Luke between discipleship and the cross. However, we must also note that the initial idea of a shared destiny even unto death has become less radical. On the one hand it comes to mean a daily readiness to deny oneself, though at the same time this idea is given a wider application. The Johannine form of the saying about winning and losing one's life, (John 12 : 25; cf. Mark 8 : 35 par.), continues as follows: 'If anyone serves me, he must follow me; and where I am, there shall my servant be also'. These sayings are given in the context of the parable of the grain of wheat which falls into the earth and must die in order to bear fruit, (12 : 24ff.).[68] This is John's way of expressing the same basic rule of discipleship. It is derived from the destiny of the Lord and Son of God who in the hour of death is raised and glorified. Luke stresses this same aspect when in his account of Paul's conversion he announces the will of the risen One: 'For I will show him how much he must suffer for the sake of my name,' (Acts 9 : 16).

In the Revelation of John (14 : 3) the image of 'the hundred and forty-four thousand' redeemed followers points to the same dialectic of suffering and life in the life of the disciple. And again the paradigm for this rule of life is the destiny of Jesus. To catch a glimpse of this action of God sets one free for the knowledge that he has won the victory in the death of Jesus and that this victory of his is one which is realised in direct opposition to the laws which govern this world.

3. *Discipleship as a Life of Service and Brotherhood.*

The idea of service, which in connection with the call to discipleship in the pre-Easter period was already of great importance, is taken up anew in the light of Easter. In John 12 : 26 discipleship is defined as service. In the story about Jesus washing the disciples' feet, (John 13 : 1ff.), the humble service of Jesus is held up as the supreme example of true discipleship: 'For I have given you an example, that you also should do as I have done to you,' (John 13 : 15).[69]

This is true of the earliest Gospel as well as of John. In Mark 10 : 42ff., which comes after the third prophecy of Jesus' suffering and which is spoken against the background of the argument between the sons of Zebedee, the nature of discipleship as service is set forth. Again this is based upon the example of Jesus' own destiny, who came as the Son of Man, not to be served but to serve and to give his life 'for many', (Mark 10 : 45).[70] It is with this theme in mind that Mark and Luke include this traditional material within the framework of the passion-story, (Mark 10 : 42ff.; Luke 22 : 24ff.).

In the Easter tradition the idea of the serving community is widened to include the idea of witnessing. As stated above, the concern of all the Evangelists is to show that the calling anew of the disciples as witnesses to the living One is grounded in the main appearance of Jesus to the disciples, (Matt. 28 : 19f.; Luke 24 : 47ff.; John 20 : 21ff.; Acts 1 : 8; Mark 16 : 15ff.; John 21 : 15ff.). For Matthew, the disciples are presented as witnesses to the Word of the earthly Jesus; for Luke, as witnesses to his suffering and to the universal offer of forgiveness; and for John, as witnesses to the Fatherhood of God as revealed in Jesus.

The image of discipleship is most profoundly described in the Gospel of John. Their relationship to the risen Lord is one of unique intimacy and complete trust. In the discourse in John 10 : 1ff., Jesus is described as the Shepherd who goes before his followers. They follow him (as his flock), 'for they know his voice'. Corresponding to the Evangelist's characteristic theme of revelation, the relationship between Lord and disciple is presented in terms of mutual recognition and of election. According to John, discipleship establishes a relationship of knowledge and trust, (cf. 10 : 27) in which the Lord bears and guards those who belong to him.[71]

The characteristics of this ideal of the disciple are of course also to be derived from the Easter stories. In response to the address of the risen One, Mary Magdalene speaks the word of recognition, Rabboni, (my master). In the appearance of Jesus on the evening of Easter Sunday, the Lord declares the disciples to be his equals: 'As the Father has sent me, even so I send you', (20 : 21). In the appendix, the commissioning to new service is rather surprisingly connected with a demand to love Jesus, (21 : 15ff.). It is rightly recognised that the story of Peter's appointment as shepherd of the sheep is not primarily meant to express his reinstatement after having formerly denied his Lord.[72] Rather it clarifies the presuppositions and circumstances as to why he should be trusted and honoured with the leadership of the community, (see also Matt. 16 : 17ff.; Luke 22 : 32). It is because he loved Jesus more than the others that he is told: 'Feed my lambs'. This comes as a result of the serious testing of Peter's love; thus his commission is at the same time connected with the total claim which is placed upon him as an apostle. Surprisingly, the story ends with Jesus' words: 'Follow me'. This obviously has two meanings. The context shows that the Lord who chooses his disciple not only calls him to unconditional service to the community, but also hints at the possibility that martyrdom may await him at the end of his service. There is no other story in the Gospels which makes the call to discipleship so radically a matter of serious personal decision.

Whenever the disciple pledges his whole self, Christian discipleship becomes more than a community of service, it becomes brotherhood. It is remarkable how strongly this idea emerges and how typical it is of the Easter-witness.

The pupil of the rabbi had to learn from his teacher and follow him. This formed part of his education. This inevitably involved subordination to the master as a necessary duty, while the pupil's own aim was that he should also become a master and gain recognition as such.[73] As far as Christian discipleship is concerned, its ultimate and exclusive aim is a community of service and of brotherhood. This understanding is most clearly expressed in Matt. 23 : 8ff. where it is twice reported that the disciple of Jesus should not call himself 'master' (rabbi). Christ alone is the Master and his followers should be brothers. The idea of brotherhood is also introduced into the Easter reports in terms of the familiar concepts of Lord and servant, Master and disciple. Christian discipleship is evidently presented as a community in which barriers are removed, and in which one bears responsibility for the other as for oneself. It

77

is in this sense that the community of disciples should live together, a community which is convinced that it is 'the new people of God'.[74] Here the idea of brotherhood plays a very prominent part. The hope expressed in Is. 66 : 20 is that when God finally gathers His people the 'brethren' from all the nations will be included. In Jeremiah's vision of the new covenant, (31 : 34), it is stated that no longer shall any man teach his 'brother' but that all men shall know the Lord. It thus appears that with the renewal of the hopes which were revived by Easter, the idea of the people of God also came to the fore and was accepted as a goal worth striving for. There is an echo of this in the Easter stories. That Paul, in 1 Cor. 15 : 6, mentions the 'five hundred brethren' is probably quite intentional.[75] With reference to the Galilee-saying, Matthew makes emphatic reference to an instruction of the risen Christ to his 'brethren', (28 : 8ff.). In a similar way the risen Christ sends instructions by Mary Magdalene to his 'brethren', (John 20 : 17). Seen in its context this phrase proves to be of considerable theological significance: 'Say to them, I am ascending to *my Father* and *your Father*'. The idea of discipleship as brotherhood is here ultimately rooted in the conviction that before God, Jesus is the Son.[76] However, the criterion of discipleship is clearly the Word and destiny of Jesus. This means that discipleship is not an imitation of Jesus but rather a following him in his obedience.[77] In order to express this in terms of our theme we may say that discipleship is to be understood as a community-in-obedience with Jesus, an obedience which is consummated in the light of the Easter-event and which stands the test of the darkness of the cross. The proclamation of Jesus would probably be meaningless today had he not himself lived it out in unconditional obedience even unto the cross. And since the message and destiny of Jesus are one, then the obedient disciple may understand himself in the light of God's same unconditional 'yes' as it is most singularly expressed in the Easter-event.

Perhaps we should emphasise this important point: the offer of discipleship and committment to it, for the disciple of Jesus, follow from God's 'yes', an affirmation witnessed to and one which can be perceived in the destiny of Jesus. This is God's paradigmatic affirmative, a 'yes' which is laden with promise for that obedience which—as with Jesus—is lived out and which remains steadfast unto death.

Notes to

DISCIPLESHIP IN THE LIGHT OF THE EASTER-EVENT

1. Cf. for further information: M. Albertz, "Zur Formgeschichte der Auferstehungsberichte", *Zeitschrift für die neutestamentliche Wissenschaft und die Kunde der älteren Kirche* (ZNW) 20, 1921, pp. 259ff.; L. Brun, *Die Auferstehung Christi in der urchristlichen Überlieferung*, 1925; J. Finegan, *Die Überlieferung der Leidens- und Auferstehungsgeschichte Jesu*, 1934; R. Bultmann, *The History of the Synoptic Tradition*, (Eng. trans. 1963). More detailed studies of the problems cannot be dealt with here.

2. E. Hirsch, *Die Auferstehungsgeschichten und der christliche Glaube*, 1940.

3. For objections to Hirsch's view, cf. among others, P. Althaus, *Die Wahrheit des christlichen Osterglaubens*, 1941, Second ed.; W. Michaelis, *Die Erscheinung des Auferstandenen*, 1944.

4. H. Grass, *Ostergeschehen und Osterberichte*, 1962, Second ed., esp. pp. 85-93 and pp. 183-186.

5. According to Grass, op. cit. p. 199f., it was only after the disciples had returned from Galilee that they heard about the discovery of the empty tomb. This view is also held by e.g. U. Wilckens, cf. note 36.

6. Op. cit. p. 107.

7. Cf. especially op. cit. pp. 233-249.

8. H. Freiherr von Campenhausen, "The Events of Easter and the Empty Tomb", in *Tradition and Life in the Church*, Collins, 1968. See especially p. 85f.

9. H. von Campenhausen, op. cit. p. 83, note 174.

10. H. von Campenhausen, op. cit. p. 86f.

11. W. Pannenberg in his book *Jesus God and Man*, p. 105f., SCM Press, 1968, emphasizes on the one hand the independent origin of the stories of the appearances, and on the other hand the tradition of the empty tomb, and pleads for the historical validity of both. A similar view is held by W. Grundmann in his book, *Die Geschichte Jesu Christi*, 1957, who gives greater historical weight to the appearances in Galilee and who also regards the story of the empty tomb as historical.

12. Cf. also H. Grass, op. cit. pp. 113-256.

13. P. Winter, *1 Corinthians XV, 3b-7, Nov. Test.*, II, 1957, pp. 142ff.

14. E.g. E. Bammel, Herkunft und Funktion der Traditionselemente in 1 Kor. 15 : 1-11, *Theol. Zeitschrift*, Basel, 1955, pp. 401-419.

15. U. Wilckens, "Die Überlieferungsgeschichte der Auferstehung Jesu", which can be found in *Die Bedeutung der Auferstehungsbotschaft für den Glauben an Jesus Christus*, Second ed. 1966, pp. 41ff. and pp. 47ff.

16. Cf. W. G. Kümmel, Kirchenbegriff und Geschichtsbewusstsein in der Urgemeinde und bei Jesus, *Symb. Bibl. Upsal.* I, 1943, pp. 2ff.; Eduard Schweizer, *Lordship and Discipleship*, p. 52.

17. This view is held e.g. by J. Jeremias, *Die Abendmahlsworte Jesu*, Third ed., 1960, pp. 95ff. (Eng. trans.: *The Eucharistic Words of Jesus*, p. 128f., Oxford, 1955); F. Hahn, *Christologische Hoheitstitel*, 1963, pp. 197-213. See also B. Klappert's recent paper "Zur Frage des semitischen oder griechischen Urtextes von 1. Kor. 15 : 3-5", in *New Test. Studies*, 13, 1966/67, pp. 168ff., which includes further references to the literature on the subject. Klappert's proof that the phrase 'for our sins' may go back to the Targum of Isaiah 53 : 5 does not help to explain the origin of the polished Greek text.

18. Eduard Schweizer, op. cit. p. 52, note 2.

19. P. Vielhauer, *Evangelische Theologie*, 25, 1965, p. 58f.

20. H. Conzelmann, "Zur Analyse der Bekenntnisformel, 1. Kor. 15 : 3-5", *Evangelische Theologie*, 25, 1965, pp. 1-11.

21. H. Conzelmann, op. cit. p. 10.

22. Cf. H. Grass, op. cit. p. 102f.; E. Lohse, "Ursprung und Prägung des christlichen Apostolats", *Theol. Zeitschrift*, 9, 1953, pp. 259ff.

23. See H. Conzelmann (note 20), and also his "Jesus von Nazareth und der Glaube an den Auferstandenen", in *Der historische Jesus und der kerygmatische Christus*, 1960, p. 188f.

24. H. Grass, op. cit. pp. 106-122, thinks that the Evangelists 'did not want to report' the other appearances (those mentioned by Paul), because they regarded them as belonging to 'the history of the young church'. In my opinion this explanation is not sufficient.

25. H. Windisch, "Die Christusepiphanie vor Damaskus und ihre religionsgeschichtlichen Parallelen", *ZNW* 31, 1932. pp. 1ff., who shows that the reports of the appearance to Paul (in Acts 9 : 22, 26), are based on a typical narrative form (similar, for example to the legend of Heliodorus).

26. This is the view of H. Grass, op. cit. pp. 85ff.

27. Cf. C. H. Dodd's recent book, *Historical Tradition in the Fourth Gospel*, 1963, pp. 137ff.

28. H. von Campenhausen, op. cit. p. 51f.

29. For the latest discussion of this problem see A. Ehrhardt, "The Disciples of Emmaus", *New Test. Studies*, 10, 1964, pp. 182ff. He makes the mistake however of not relating the text of the pericope with Luke.

30. The best proof of this is Paul's own life. Cf. G. Klein, "Die Zwölf Apostel, Ursprung und Gehalt einer Idee", *FRILANT*, N. F., 59, 1961, pp. 40ff.

31. With reference to this see e.g. R. Bultmann, *The History of the Synoptic Tradition*, p. 287, commenting on Mark 16 : 1-8.

Against this view see W. Nauck's, "Die Bedeutung des leeren Grabes für den Glauben an den Auferstandenen", *ZNW* 47, 1956, pp. 243ff. and p. 256, who says that 'it acted neither as a proof of the resurrection nor was it to evoke faith in the risen Christ, nor was it intended as an official report'.

32. Towards the beginning of Semachoth 8 it says: 'Everyone goes

out to the place of burial to view the dead for up to three days . . .'
(Strack-Billerbeck I, p. 1048). According to Gen. R. 100 (64a): 'Bar
Qappara has taught: "Mourning reaches its height on the third day. For
three days the soul returns to the grave. It thinks that it will return (to the
body)" '.

33. This verse is given in all groups of MSS. (also Papyrus 75) except
Codex D, the Itala MSS. and Marcion. The reason why this verse is
missing in Codex D is because it contains a harmonizing tradition which is
dependent on Tatian and throughout replaced Luke 24 : 12 by John
20 : 3ff. (This is also the case with the Arabian, Persian, Old High German
and Old Italian Diatessaron tradition.) The influence of Tatian is probably
also to be found in the Itala MSS. It was for obvious dogmatic reasons
that Marcion left the verse out. (Translator's note: Readers are referred to
the text of the AV in connection with this note. See also RSV and the
comment on Luke 24 : 12, v.)

34. Luke 24 : 12 is generally held to be a resumé of John 20 : 3ff.,
and is said to have been later inserted into the Lukan text, (see H. Grass,
op. cit. p. 54, and others). According to the history of the text itself there
are no grounds for this opinion, (see note 33). John 20 : 3ff. certainly
presupposes the Lukan verse and corrects it by introducing the 'other
disciple'. In my view this correction is based upon a better knowledge of
the sequence of events, and is not the adoption of a position in relation to
the Johannine and Petrine rivalry in the early church and with regard to
the two eponyms, (see R. Bultmann, *Meyer Kommentar*, II, Fourteenth
Rd., p. 531).

35. Pierre Benoit in "Marie-Madeleine et les Disciples au Tombeau
selon Jean 20 : 1-18", in *Judentum, Urchristentum, Kirche*, Festschrift
für J. Jeremias, *BZNW* 26, 1960, pp. 141ff., regards verse 12 as Lukan,
but assumes that it has been taken from the Gospel of John and inserted
into Luke's Gospel. G. Hartmann, in "Die Vorlage der Osterberichte in
Joh. 20", in *ZNW* 55, 1964, pp. 197ff., takes a similar view as regards this
dependent relationship, but also regards it as secondary. The verse is very
similar indeed to the Lukan style, cf. e.g. the pre-birth stories, (2 : 15, *to
gegonòs*; 8 : 34; 2 : 18: *thaumázein*; 2 : 33; but always with a preposition).

36. H. von Campenhausen also rightly objects to this view, op. cit.
p. 78f. (He and others refer to the view that the disciples fled to Galilee as
'a legend created by the critics'). All attempts at reconstruction which are
based on the assumption that the disciples fled to Galilee, soon become
lost in vague speculation. Cf. e.g. U. Wilckens, *Die Überlieferungsgeschichte* . . . p. 61: 'It was the appearances of the risen Christ in Galilee
which evoked the Easter faith and thereby constituted the early community.
Having moved back to Jerusalem the early community learned about the
report of the women and how they had discovered the empty tomb. This
acted as a confirmation of the resurrection-faith which they had already
found. . . .'

37. H. W. Bartsch, "Parusieerwartung und Osterbotschaft", *Evangelische Theologie*, 1947/48, pp. 115ff.; E. Grässer, "Das Problem der
Parusieverzögerung in den synopt. Evangelien und in der Apostel-

geschichte", *BZNW* 22, 1957, p. 59, (Second ed. 1960); H. W. Bartsch, "Zum Problem der Parusieverzögerung", *Evangelische Theol.* 19, 1959, pp. 116ff.

38. W. Pannenberg, *Jesus God and Man*, SCM Press, p. 96, for example, thinks that it took some considerable time before the early community realised that 'with the resurrection, the end had not yet come for everyone'. The message of Easter as the report of an event which had happened only to Jesus was something which slowly emerged within the framework of the apocalyptic tradition.

39. Cf. R. Bultmann, "Ist die Apokalyptik die Mutter christlicher Theologie?" in *Apophoreta*, Festschrift für Ernst Haenchen, 1964, p. 64. More accurate is the view of G. Klein, see "Römer 4 und die Idee der Heilsgeschichte", *Evangelische Theologie*, 23, 1963, pp. 425ff.

40. Cf. W. Thüsing, "Die Erhöhung und Verherrlichung Jesu im Johannesevangelium", *Neutestamentliche Abhandlungen* XX, 1. 2, 1960, p. 99f., 289ff. etc. The eschatological significance of Jesus' death is rightly pointed out.

41. W. Marxsen, "Die Auferstehung Jesu als historisches und als theologisches Problem", 1964; Reprinted in *Die Bedeutung der Auferstehungsbotschaft für den Glauben an Jesus Christus*, Gütersloh, 1966, Second ed., pp. 9ff.

42. On these grounds W. Marxsen may also be criticised. Cf. "Erwägungen zum Problem des verkündigten Kreuzes", *New Test. Studies* 8, 1961/62, pp. 204ff. W. Marxsen demands that the proclamation of Good Friday should not point towards Easter, but from Easter towards the present.

43. The same point is raised by F. Gogarten in *Jesus Christus, Wende der Welt, Grundfragen zur Christologie*, 1966, pp. 58ff. Gogarten rightly says: 'Nevertheless, because Jesus obediently surrenders to this nothingness, it is no longer the nothingness which seeks to assert itself against God or the nothingness of the world as independent of His 'eternal power and deity'. Just as it is true that the eternal will of God is powerfully active in the obedience of Jesus and in the responsibility with which he takes this nothingness upon Himself, so it is also true that the Crucified becomes 'the first-born from the dead', (Col. 1 : 18).

44. Cf. W. G. Kümmel, "Jesus und Paulus", in *Heilsgeschehen und Geschichte*, Gesammelte Aufsätze 1933-1964, 1965, pp. 439ff.

45. W. C. Till, "Die gnostischen Schriften des kopt. Papyrus Berol. 8502", *Texte und Untersuchungen zur Geschichte der altchristlichen Literatur (TU)* 60, 1955, p. 79.

46. W. C. Till, op. cit. pp. 195ff.

47. With reference to this, cf. H. Grass op. cit. pp.116ff. (and Appendix), who shows little understanding for the eschatological situation of the disciples.

48. Cf. also e.g. John 16 : 16: 'Again a little while, and you will see me'.

49. This is the view taken by W. Marxsen in *Der Evangelist Markus*, 1959, Second ed., pp. 66ff. According to M. Karnetzki, "Die Galiläische Redaktion im Markusev.", *ZNW* 52, 1961, pp. 238ff. Mark 14 : 28 and 16 : 7 have no reference to the Parousia but rather to the departure to Galilee in order to preach and to carry out their mission, (p. 256).

50. The widespread way in which one tends to refer to a 'departure for the Parousia' is really misleading. It was not the 'coming' but the 'appearing' which was the actual content of the hope.

51. Cf. G. Bornkamm, "Der Auferstandene und der Irdische", (Matt. 28 : 16-20) in *Zeit und Geschichte*, Dankesgabe an R. Bultmann zum 80. Geburtstag, 1964, pp. 171ff.

52. Cf. E. Lohse, *Die Auferstehung Jesu Christi im Zeugnis des Lukas-evangeliums*, 1961.

53. H. Grass. op. cit. p. 60, ('a variation of Matt. 28 : 9f.').

54. Cf. J. Jeremias, *Jesu Verheissung für die Völker*, 1958 (Eng. trans.: *Jesus' Promise to the Nations*, SCM Studies in Biblical Theology, No. 24, 1958). For my own view, cf. A. Strobel, *Kerygma und Apokalyptik*, 1967; and *Die moderne Jesusforschung*, Calwer Hefte, 83, 1966.

55. Paul places exclusive emphasis on the 'seeing', (cf. 1 Cor. 9 : 1, 15 : 8; also Gal. 1 : 16). In the later Lukan reports concerning the vision on the road to Damascus, the question of a bodily resurrection is probably intentionally left out. The later tradition differs: 'which we have looked upon . . . touched with our hands'. (1 John 1 : 1).

56. With reference to the notion of exaltation P. Vielhauer writes: 'There are no grounds for asserting that it (the idea of exaltation) does not belong to the primitive Palestinian community. The earliest reports concerning this community, the fact that they assembled in Jerusalem, their mission to the Jews, all this presupposes a conviction about the presence of the One who has ascended and been enthroned, and the prayer, "Maranatha" also presupposes the "exaltation" of Jesus.' ("Ein Weg zur neutestamentliche Christologie?" in *Aufsätze zum Neuen Testament*, Theol. Bücherei 31, 1956, pp. 162ff., 167ff., 175). Cf. also E. Schweizer, *Lordship and Discipleship*, pp. 32ff., pp. 68ff.

57. Cf. also G. Delling, "Der Tod Jesu in der Verkündigung des Paulus", in *Apophoreta*, pp. 85ff. For the more recent theological discussion see the informative collection of essays edited by B. Klappert: *Diskussion um Kreuz und Auferstehung*, 1967. I would like to emphasize in particular the helpful remarks of H. J. Iwand, (pp. 275ff. and 279ff.), whose exposition is very close to my own.

58. Cf. E. Schweizer, "Zur Frage des Messiasgeheimnisses bei Markus", *ZNW* 56, 1965, pp. 1ff., p. 8; also U. Luz, "Das Geheimnismotiv und die markin. Christologie", in the same volume, pp. 9ff.

59. Cf. note 51.

60. Cf. note 52, and also E. Lohse, "Lukas als Theologe der Heilsge-schichte", in *Evangelische Theol.* 1954, pp. 256ff.; E. Grässer, op. cit. pp. 178ff. and 204ff.; W. C. Robinson, *Der Weg des Herrn, Studien zur Geschichte und Eschatologie im Lukasevangelium*, 1964; H. Hegermann, "Zur Theologie des Lukas", in *Sie fragten nach Jesus*, Festschrift für E. Barnikol zum 70, Geburtstag, 1964, pp. 27ff., (who is critical of the one-sided 'heilsgeschichtlich' interpretation of Luke).

61. E. Schweizer, *Lordship and Discipleship*, p. 134f. A. Schulz, *Nachfolgen und Nachahmen*, Studien über das Verhältnis der neutesta-mentlichen Jüngerschaft zur urchristlichen Vorbildethik, Stud. z. Alten und Neuen Test. 6, 1962, pp. 137ff.

62. Cf. Gal. 1 : 16. On the subjective-psychological factors see, H. Grass, op. cit. pp. 238ff. and pp. 247ff. Also A. Strobel, Article 'Vision' (NT) in Die Religion in Geschichte und Gegenwart, Third ed.

63. This however is the view of R. Bultmann, *Johanneskommentar*, p. 530, note 10.

64. Cf. H. Conzelmann, Jesus von Nazareth und der Glaube an den Auferstandenen, in *Der historische Jesus und der kerygmatische Christus*, pp. 188ff., p. 199.

65. Cf. E. Schweizer, *Lordship and Discipleship*, pp. 126ff.

66. Cf. E. Kamlah, "Wie beurteilt Paulus sein Leiden?" *ZNW* 54, 1963, pp. 217ff.

67. Cf. also E. Larsson, *Christus als Vorbild, Eine Untersuchung zu den paulinischen Tauf- und Eikontexten*, Uppsala, 1962, pp. 40ff.; E. Schweizer, *Lordship and Discipleship*, pp. 11ff., whose concern is to work out the pre-Easter content.

68. Cf. C. H. Dodd, *Historical Tradition*, pp. 338ff.; E. Larsson, op. cit. pp. 42ff.; E. Schweizer, op. cit. p. 77.

69. Cf. R. Bultmann, *Johanneskommentar*, p. 358: 'He whom Jesus has served shares a common destiny with him. . . .'

70. Cf. J. Jeremias, "Das Lösegeld für Viele, (Mark 10 : 45)", in *Abba, Studien zur neutestamentlichen Theologie und Zeitgeschichte*, 1966, pp. 216ff., pp. 224ff.

71. Cf. also E. Schweizer, *Lordship and Discipleship*, p. 82.

72. This is rightly seen by R. Bultmann, *Johanneskommentar*, p. 551.

73. Cf. K-H. Rengstorf, Art. "mathetes", in *Kittel-Friedrich, Theologisches Wörterbuch*, IV, pp. 434ff., 552.

74. Cf. W. G. Kummel, "Jesus und die Anfange der Kirche", in *Heilsgeschehen und Geschichte*, pp. 289ff., 294ff., 309.

75. According to H. Grass, op. cit. p. 98: 'Apparently, people . . . who belonged to the new post-Easter community'. This contrasts with the views of others who identify this group with the Pentecost community.

76. R. Bultmann, *Johanneskommentar*, p. 533f. With reference to this see J. Jeremias, *Abba*, in *Abba, Studien zur neutestamentlichen Theologie*, pp. 15ff., 33ff.

77. Cf. also E. Schweizer, *Erniedrigung und Erhöhung*, pp. 159ff. (Eng. trans.: *Lordship and Discipleship*.)

Discipleship and Church

By EDUARD SCHWEIZER

I

WITH regard to the question of the continuity between discipleship and church we must first of all take into consideration the fact that Jesus' sayings about discipleship became part of the tradition of the post-Easter church. Nor were the reasons for this purely historical. Jesus' call to discipleship, as we find it in Mark 1 : 16-20 and in 2 : 14, is described in a way which has the simplicity and clarity of a woodcut. Unimportant things are left aside, descriptions of accompanying circumstances, indications as to time and place, or more detailed descriptions of those involved, are lacking. The whole scene has actually been called an 'ideal scene', created by the later community in order to present its own conception of discipleship. In both contexts the emphasis is upon the authoritative action of Jesus. Man's response is said to occur almost as a matter of course. Jesus sees man as God sees him, (Mark 1 : 16 and 19; 2 : 14; 10 : 21; Luke 19 : 5; John 1 : 48), that is, he chooses him, (cf. 1 Sam. 16 : 1). He calls him and he will make him a fisher of men. Man is entirely unprepared for this. He is in the midst of his daily occupation. All that is said about his discipleship is that he followed and not even the slightest hint is given concerning the difficulties which this might have involved for himself or for others.

Even in the two sayings about discipleship which are derived from the sayings-source, (Matt. 8 : 19-22), it is Jesus' authority alone which is stressed. He is much more important than the father who died and whose burial was considered to be the primary duty. He is also the Son of Man whose call involves a life which is poorer and lowlier than that of the foxes and the birds, yet who nevertheless calls his disciple with authority to exactly this kind of life which he himself lives. Of course, the people who are described here are people who wanted to follow Jesus. But at the same time it is quite clear that the human wish to follow is not enough. It is true that nothing is said about whether or not the two questioners responded to Jesus' call; this aspect of the pericope is not decisive. But in any case, these sayings of Jesus are meant to illustrate just how little man knows about the meaning of discipleship. Luke 9 : 61 and the additional verse 62 about putting one's hand to the plough is the only instance where the attitude of the disciple is described. However, it is quite clear that here Luke has first composed verse 61 and has placed this saying within the framework of a story about discipleship. Even the story of the Rich Man who refuses to risk giving up all his possessions (Mark 10 : 17-22), emphasises that the most important thing is to seize the moment when God comes to us in Jesus and to regard this as the most decisive event of all. It applies to this situation as well that to give away all one's possessions is not a condition which must first of all be fulfilled, rather, it is precisely the way in which in this instance discipleship is meant to be lived. The casual and almost incidental enumeration at the beginning of the well-known commandments, to which Jesus gives no newer or more radical interpretation, already shows that Jesus' intention is not to lay down the conditions which man must first of all fulfil. His concern is rather to give him joy so that he may embark upon the path of obedience with God, a way to which at the same time he is totally bound. Nor did the community hesitate to relate those accounts in which Jesus had not called men to discipleship in this way. An instance of this is when Jesus sends the healed Gerasene demoniac who wanted to follow him, back to his family, (Mark 5 : 19). At the same time, a man like this still belongs wholly to Jesus.

If we examine the Synoptic pericopes about discipleship as a whole and in the form in which they have come down to us, then it may be said that in them the post-Easter church saw primarily the authority of Jesus, the authority with which God came to men and called them out of their old ties and so began to shape their lives from that moment on. The community realised that what had happened in Jesus was God's act of grace, the event in which the reign of God came upon men, made them whole, and called them to obedience. This is precisely what happened when in Jesus' historical action he called Levi for example, away from the table of custom, or Peter and Andrew away from their nets, to the life of discipleship. And this is what happens again and again whenever Jesus establishes his reign over men, whenever he makes men whole and calls them to a new obedience. God's salvation and man's obedience belong together. The only thing which can really make a man whole is the experience that God means *him* so seriously that his obedience to God is no longer of little consequence but of infinite importance. For salvation consists in the fact that God can use and wishes to use the service of man, and God gives man the ability, the power, and the goodwill to fulfil this service.

II

We shall deal with each Evangelist individually. It can quite easily be shown for example, how Mark, the composer of the second Gospel, gives a central place to discipleship within the whole framework of the Gospel. In Mark this theme is of extreme importance. At the beginning of the Gospel, Jesus first of all proclaims the kingdom of God, and this is immediately followed by his call to discipleship, (Mark 1 : 14-20). The second instance, (2 : 14, the call of Levi), comes before the sayings which point out the dangers of legalism and the way in which such dangers should be met.

The pericope Mark 8 : 27 to 9 : 1 is also of special importance. It is clear that, for Mark, Peter's confession is, as such, of no particular significance. Peter has not even reached the stage of the demons who, according to 3 : 11 and 5 : 7, already know perfectly well who Jesus is, namely, the Son of God. Nor does Jesus in any way deny that he is the Christ. However, his immediate reaction to the disciples almost takes the form of a threat; they are to tell no one about this, and putting the whole discussion into its proper perspective he tells them that the Son of Man must suffer, (Mark 8 : 31). It is only now that the real point is made and this can be seen from the short sentence in 32a. Here Mark, employing a formula which has already appeared twice, says that only now does Jesus proclaim the Word to them openly and no longer in parables, as in 4 : 33. And it is to this first direct revelation of God that Peter responds with complete misunderstanding, (v. 33). Jesus can only emphasise all the more (cf. v. 34ff.) the discipleship of the One who must go to the cross, in the light of which the mystery of the suffering of the Son of Man is alone to be understood. It is clear that Mark separates these verses from the preceding one because the latter are addressed to all. Discipleship is therefore not merely something for specially chosen people. Everyone is called, so that as disciples they may understand the meaning of God's revelation, (v. 31).

In these sayings concerning discipleship it is stated that only the man who finds himself in giving his life can understand what Jesus has openly said about God in his saying about the suffering of the Son of Man. The conclusion is reached in 8 : 38 and 9 : 1 with the references to the end of all things and the judgement. To the present writer this seems to indicate that Mark's eschatology functions primarily as a background to the calls to discipleship. And this is meant to show how important it is that one should follow Jesus today.

It can easily be shown how the passage from 8 : 27 to 10 : 52, from the moment at Caesarea Philippi to the entry into Jerusalem, is characterised by the discipleship theme. There are three announcements of suffering; three times the disciples misunderstand, and three times Jesus speaks about true discipleship. This whole sequence comes to an end with the healing of the blind man in Jericho of whom it is said: 'And he followed him on the way'. (These are the last words before the entry into Jerusalem and the story of the passion.) The key phrase 'on the way' has already appeared in verse 32 where it quite clearly refers to the way up to Jerusalem. This is discipleship described at its most radical and it is in this section that there is also to be found the story of the Rich Man to which we have already referred. However, this whole section also gives a description of the failure of the disciples, a theme which becomes so important afterwards in the passion story itself. Nevertheless, the Gospel comes to an end with the promise spoken almost in the same moment as the prophecy of

Peter's denial, the promise that Jesus will once again go before them to Galilee, (Mark 14 : 28, and again 16 : 7). Here it is stated again that only the miracle of the resurrection can make discipleship at all possible because this leads to the Exalted Christ going before his disciples, the disciples who had denied him.

We now go on to examine Matthew and especially his version of Peter's confession, (16 : 13ff.). From the post-Easter point of view it now appears that this recognition of the Christ has become so fundamental that the promise is made that upon this confession of Peter the church will be built. The problem of the church as distinct from all the nations, an idea which in this form did not occur in the preaching of Jesus, will be dealt with in section IV. Matthew emphasises however that this recognition of the Christ and discipleship itself are basically gifts. However, from verse 21ff. the Markan account to which we have already referred is taken up.

Finally with regard to Luke, and especially 5 : 1ff. which deals with the call of Peter, it can be shown how the post-Easter community again stresses the gift-character of this event, just like the gift which was actually received by Levi the publican, a man who did not belong to the people of God, when Jesus called him again to his service. The same is shown here also when Peter confesses that he is a sinful man, and when Jesus says to him: 'Do not be afraid', and then takes him into his service as a fisher of men. Here again the story ends with the words: 'They left everything', (v. 11), which once more is understood not as an achievement of man, but as the gift of God.

Let us now examine this in John's version of it because it is here that we can see most clearly how the post-Easter community understood the meaning of discipleship. In 1 : 35-51 (par. Mark 1 : 16-20), which describes the call of the first disciples, the new concern of the post-Easter church is already quite apparent. To harmonise these two reports and to try and fit them together into a coherent sequence of events by treating John 1 as the first encounter and Mark 1 as a later encounter, something which has frequently been attempted before, would be to miss the point of both and to destroy their message. We would miss the whole point which both John and

Mark in their own way are trying to make. In the case of Mark, the proclamation of the unprecedented and mysterious authority of God in Jesus would be destroyed if we were to assume only that the disciples simply responded to his call because they had had ample opportunity beforehand to meet him, and sufficient time to consider whether it would be worth following him or not. And in John's case we would find it impossible to recognise the fact that in telling this story he is quite obviously and quite emphatically concerned with the situation of the church in his own day. The concept of discipleship occurs four times, (verses 37, 38, 40 and 43) and here there are some considerable differences when we compare this with the older stories about discipleship.

The first rather striking thing about John 1 : 35-51 is that it is no longer Jesus himself who calls men to be disciples. This is also the case even in verse 43, although according to the present text it is not clear whether it is Jesus or Peter who finds Philip. However it is most likely that originally it was always the witness to Jesus who issued the call. It is John the Baptist who, witnessing to Jesus as the Lamb of God, directs the first disciples to him; and again and again it is always the one who is called who finds someone else and then sends him to Jesus. This is John's way of emphasising that the call of Jesus continues to sound forth in the post-Easter church. For it is quite obvious that the historical Jesus no longer walks among the communities of John's own time. This means that the call is no longer the call of the earthly Jesus but the call of his witness.

The second point we may note is that all those who testify to Jesus give a clear and explicit witness to him which describes his significance in dogmatic terms. He is the Lamb of God who takes away the sin of the world, (John 1 : 29 and 36). This is in fact the proper translation. There is no reference here to the apocalyptic ram who sweeps away the sin of the world in his judgement as has been suggested. Jesus is the Messiah, (John 1 : 41), of whom Moses had written in the Law and to whom the prophets also bore witness, (John 1 : 45). The unprecedented and overwhelming authority of God which comes with Jesus is no longer an event which simply takes place in an encounter between him and the one who is called to discipleship. It is mediated through the witness of the preacher. He has to testify to the encounter with this authority which he himself has experienced. There is no final formula for this experience which might simply be recited by others, for if there were, it would no longer be a genuine testimony. Each one describes it in a different way and in terms most appropriate to himself. Nevertheless, they all witness to that which is ultimate, that which can only be hinted at as a mystery and which cannot be defined.

The third point concerns that which the disciple leaves behind. Here there is a recognition of new possibilities as well as new dangers. It is no longer the fishing-boat and the table of custom which have to be left behind, because now the community has rightly learned that in general they will not be called away from these things in order to live the kind of life which consists mainly in wandering from one place to another. But if Jesus is to remain the risen and living Lord of the church and not a dead historical figure, then he must always continue to call the community away from those things which might destroy it or hinder its service or stand in the way of its joyous relationship to God, just as he had called people away from similar things during his earthly life. In John 1 the things from which men must be called away by Jesus are always those other 'saviours', or certain dogmatic ideas in which until now men have tried to find their salvation. It is not John the Baptist that men should follow, but Jesus. Here we may recall how strong an emphasis there is in this Gospel on the contrast between John the Baptist, whom some regarded as a saviour-figure, and Jesus, (cf. John 1 : 6-8, 19-27; 3 : 22-30 etc.). He who matters now is neither Moses nor the Prophets but the One whom they had promised. What now matters is no longer the dogmatic, and even exegetically established prejudice that no salvation can come out of Nazareth, but the knowledge that it is God's will that it should come about in this way.

Even so, it is not forgotten that it is still Jesus who issues the call and who offers the gift of discipleship. The only difference is that John has to develop in a much more elaborate way that which took place in Jesus' life in one single act. It is always the case that the call of the witness can only send a person on his way, on that way upon which he then encounters Jesus for himself. Then he is won over by him, for he can now see in Jesus that to which the witness can only testify and that for which the witness can provide no visible proofs. According to the text, those disciples who have set out on the way through the witness of John, go and remain with Jesus for a time. In remaining with him they are won over. To the sceptical Nathaniel the witness merely says: 'Come and see'. This is an indication of the remarkable freedom which the witness has in the performance of his task. His duty is to testify and he must justify his testimony by his entire conduct. However, it is also part of his duty to lead the other to Jesus and that he should not trust in his own ability to convince him. This is the reason why Philip does not enter into any discussion with Nathaniel, though no doubt he could quite easily have quoted various texts to show that God had frequently chosen the small and the unlikely, and that he could therefore, for example, also choose the little town of Nazareth, just in the same way as great prophets had come from unknown and insignificant places, like Amos from Tekoa. A striking thing is also the sense of freedom which comes when men here believe in the continuing authority of the risen One, who himself wins over those who have been sent on the way to him by the witness. They will indeed see that which the witness can only speak about.

John does not omit the fact that discipleship means obedience, or rather, the discipleship becomes obedience. When in 12 : 26 it says that the disciple will always be where Jesus himself is, then this also means sharing the glory of God. This is again clearly indicated in 17 : 24. However, in the context of chapter 12, verse 24 refers to the death of Jesus and compares it with the death of a grain of wheat, and in verse 25 it is stated (and it is deliberately left open whether the words are spoken by Jesus himself or by a disciple) that only he who hates his life will keep it for eternal life. In the next reference similar to this, (13 : 36 to 14 : 6), it is clearly emphasised that such obedience, which in certain circumstances might well lead to martyrdom, is never possible to men in their own power but is always the gift of Jesus himself. Peter, who imagines that all one requires in order to remain with Jesus is courage and resolution unto death, has to accept the fact that he is unable to travel on this way before Jesus himself has completed it.

This will also become for Peter the Way, the Truth and the Life, the way which at the same time will lead to the heavenly mansions. And it is the risen One also who in 21 : 18f. makes a prophecy to Peter about his martyrdom and who calls him to discipleship. However, in the same passage, in verses 19-22, it is evident that the disciple whom Jesus loved is also a true disciple, though it is said that he shall not suffer martyrdom.

The extent to which the literal idea of following is still connected with that of 'discipleship' can be seen from these passages. Following begins in that moment when the risen One calls Peter in Galilee who then literally takes a few steps and follows him, though in this case there is no longer the intention of going together to any definite or particular place within Galilee. When we take into account the very individual interpretation which John gives, we can see that his concern here is also to show that Jesus establishes his reign and binds the disciple to himself in absolute obedience. Here this is also his act of grace. And here it is expressly stated—in order to counter certain misunderstandings which had arisen in the meantime—that man is unable to become a discile in his own strength, not even a Peter. Above all, it is described how in the post-Easter period, the call comes to the hearer by means of the proclamation of the witness, and also how the hearer chooses to remain in the presence of Jesus so that he is then won over by him.

Another aspect of the call of Jesus and one which formed part of its original structure also stands out, namely, that this call to respond to the reign of God and the call to obedience means such salvation for men that any other salvation which might be offered by other 'saviours' or which might be said to consist in the acceptance of certain dogmatic propositions pales into insignificance. It is quite obvious that salvation is not contained simply in a dogmatic concept to which one must give one's intellectual assent and thus know that one is thereby saved. It is rather an actual experience in which life finds its fulfilment. It is for this reason that every witness must describe it anew in his own words. Grace as a mere concept is as meaningless as an 'Abracadabra', or any other word for that matter, unless one can give some indication as to what this grace really means. In John's words the answer is that grace

93

means living with Jesus. Here grace becomes manifest in actual following, in the self-denial which can amount to hating one's own life and which may even lead to martyrdom, but which also means sharing the glory of the Father, the expression of eternal life.

III

It is rather more difficult to describe the way in which Paul has taken up the sayings and stories about discipleship. With Paul it is not the case that these sayings and stories are once again simply re-formulated in order to indicate to the community how discipleship continues to live on in its new situation. It is for this reason that terms such as 'to follow' and words like 'disciple' are no longer to be found in Paul's writings. Instead of these terms we find statements such as 'to be crucified', 'buried' and 'risen with Christ'.

According to Matthew 26 : 35, Peter has already spoken about dying with Christ; according to Luke 8 : 38 the disciple wishes to be with him, and in 22 : 56 it is said of Peter that he was with him. There are also those formulations which use the Greek word *meta* (with) instead of *sun* (which also means 'with' and which is used by Paul). In all three of the above instances *sun* is the preposition which is used. We should also consider such texts as Mark 3 : 14, according to which the Twelve are chosen so that they might be with him; also the saying: 'he who is not with me is against me,' (Matt. 12 : 30), and certain episodes such as keeping watch with him in the Garden of Gethsemane, (Matt. 26 : 36-40), continuing with him in his trials, (Luke 22 : 28), the promise to the thief who was crucified with him that he will be with him in paradise, (Luke 23 : 43), and finally in the Fourth Gospel sayings such as those which refer to dying with him, (John 11 : 16), being with him from the beginning, (John 15 : 27), and being with him in the glory of the Father, (John 17 : 24). In these texts *meta* is used.

However, does not Paul himself say that all this has already taken place in baptism? Does this therefore not mean that something quite different from the older sayings about discipleship is meant here? This certainly poses some serious problems. But first of all I must make one or two remarks with regard to language.[1]

We shall be with Christ (*sun Christo*) above all after the return of Jesus, or, speaking in terms of the individual we shall be with him after death, (1 Thess. 4 : 14 and 17; Phil. 1 : 23 etc.). According to the most precise formulations of Paul, he speaks about life *in* Christ now, and life *with* Christ in the consummation. This particular usage has no immediate connection with the sayings about discipleship but is derived more from the Old Testament and from late Jewish texts. The eschatological reign of God proves itself in that we shall live a life of fulfilment *with* Christ. However, since the ministry of John the Baptist, baptism was understood as an anticipation of the end, and in my view, there are a considerable number of indications that the pre-Pauline, and the Pauline community itself, understood baptism in this way. At first there was an attempt to interpret baptism as containing the promise, and eventually even the guarantee, of a future entrance into the reign of God. However, the enthusiasts in Corinth took the view that by being baptised one was made divine, that one had already risen with Christ and was living the eschatological life with Christ. There can be no doubt that an enthusiasm of this kind lived on for a quite considerable time. We can see this, for example, in the case of Hymenaeus and Philetus, who declared that the resurrection had already taken place, and who for this belief were strictly admonished by the author of 2 Timothy, (2 : 17f.). In circles such as these it was probably declared that the eschatological life with Christ, which is an Old Testament-Jewish conception, was something which began with baptism, and that the believer had already risen with Christ. It is against this dangerous kind of enthusiasm that Paul fights when he speaks about being crucified and buried with Christ, of a future rising with Christ, or of a rising with Christ which is to be understood in terms of the moral life.

It is interesting to consider what Paul is doing here. The theological difficulties which this problem posed for him are sufficiently clear. As regards the Corinthians, he has to stress the fact that the resurrection and the idea of being transferred into the life of the end-time have not yet taken place. They still live in this world and not simply in the eschatological reign of God. On the other hand, however, he also wishes to stress the fact that baptism does mean a quite decisive change. Thus in Rom. 6 : 2ff. he says that all of us who have been crucified with Christ have died to sin that we might walk in newness of life. The resurrection-life is therefore a task which is meant to be taken up and lived, a life which should authenticate itself in the daily life of the community.

What is it then that has in fact really happened? Is it something which is to be understood only in purely human terms? Is it simply a resolution to the effect that one is willing to live a new life; or a resolution that one is willing to obey? It is at this point that Paul takes up precisely that aspect which was implied in Jesus' call to discipleship and which was developed in different ways by the Synoptics and by John. For Paul the two aspects involved are quite clear: it is the death of Jesus upon which this change is based and which in fact effects the change. We are baptised into his death. This means that the person who is baptised is really dead to sin and that being crucified, buried and dead with Christ is something which becomes manifest in the life of such a person. The death of Jesus which Paul carries in the body, (2 Cor. 4 : 10), is as real as the marks of the whip on his back. It is manifest in his hunger and thirst, in shipwreck and persecution, in scourgings and imprisonment. For Paul, to follow Jesus is as real as this. In this way he dies daily with Christ, (Rom. 8 : 36; 1 Cor. 15 : 30). Thus for Paul the future glory with Christ involves suffering with him in the present, (Rom. 8 : 17; cf. also Phil. 3 : 10 and later 2 Tim. 2 : 11f.). Yet this in itself shows that it is no longer he who lives, but Christ in him. And this means being crucified with Christ, (Gal. 2 : 19f.). This is where Paul emphasises that all this has happened because Jesus has given himself for him, and not simply because Paul himself has resolved to live a new life, nor because he has decided to believe that this is true, nor because he has come to the decision that he should open himself to this promise. As Ernst Käsemann has pointed out,[2] this can be understood only when it is recognised that God's new righteousness comes to reign over men, and that justification by faith means precisely to be placed under this new reign.

Here a category is taken up in terms of which alone Jesus' call to discipleship is to be understood. God's gracious action consists precisely in the fact that he calls a man to his service. When someone says: 'You are a very nice person. I like you and you have many good qualities', this can hardly be called grace. Only when someone calls us to a task, in the performance of which we can be of real service, only then can we speak of grace. This is what salvation means: that man is taken out of the lostness of his own world into communion with God. Grace means that man's whole life is now seen under the light of grace itself. And it is in this sense that Paul can say that with the death and resurrection of Jesus, God's new reign has in fact been established.

This is something which can be spoken of only in the indicative, that is to say, something which can only be proclaimed. The situation is similar to that of the liberator having finally driven out the former occupying forces and set up his own rule. The fact remains that a reign is now established which is different in kind. It is not to be described in terms of those facts which, for example, can be established about a meteor which has fallen to the earth. Such a meteor could lie in some desert for thousands of years without anyone knowing about it. When someone discovers it there then begins the detached research of the scientist who regards this meteor simply as an object to be examined. But as far as any reign is concerned, it is something which is quite inconceivable without a people. A reign necessarily implies a people who live under such a reign. One may be for it or against it. One can either put oneself at the disposal of the lord who rules or oppose him, and between these two poles there are many other possibilities. But in one sense or the other, conduct is always determined by the fact of this reign and takes on its own special character even though I may act as though it did not exist. In this sense, Jesus, in exercising his rule, always creates man's obedience or brands his disobedience as rebellion. Thus, since the crossing of the Red Sea, every Israelite is *per se* an Israelite and is therefore distinct from an Egyptian or an Assyrian. From the very beginning his conduct is stamped as being either obedient or disobedient. He either gives God praise or gives way to resignation, according to whatever the case may be. Thus in a new way Paul has taken up that which was already true for the disciples of Jesus. It is wholly God's act of grace in Jesus which establishes the new reign and which thereby brings salvation to men. This occurs in such a way that the man who has received God's grace is led on the way with Jesus, to live and to suffer with him, and also finally to be glorified with him.

IV

It is quite true that in the period which separates the first disciples of Jesus from the church of the age of Paul or John, and from that time right down to the present, many dangers have been apparent and many mistakes made. But it should be remembered that this is how it has to be, because the mere repetition of a saying of Jesus or the mere reporting of any episode which took place in the past can never guarantee that in the newer circumstances of a later time the opposite meaning of what was originally intended might not be taken.[3] At the same time we also have to assert the opposite of this. We have to return again and again to those sayings and stories in order to examine our own interpretations, and whether the meaning we discover is the right one.

We can only give a very brief sketch of this. For the disciples who had fled from Gethsemane and who had probably left Jerusalem altogether, the whole affair with Jesus was at an end. As far as they were concerned, anything that took place from this point on could no longer be considered the action of God. It was Jesus himself who marked the new beginning by appearing as the risen One to his disciples. What had taken place earlier, when they were first called, happened again. He came to them as the One who had already established his reign and who now called them to obedience. One of the few things that can be ascertained is that the disciples, under the reign of the exalted Christ, apparently left Galilee for good and settled in Jerusalem together with their families. It was then that they also understood the command of the risen Christ concerning the necessity for mission, a mission which eventually spread out beyond the borders of Israel.

One interesting point is that in spite of this, the community at first understood itself as still living within the Jewish nation, and tolerated such things as the priesthood, the cult of sacrifice, synagogue-worship and the Law. It was clear to them from their understanding of Jesus and his ministry that their duty was not to form a special group within the Jewish nation, nor were they meant to offer some other variety of religious practice as did the Pharisees or the people of Qumran. It was Israel as a whole which was called into the coming kingdom, the kingdom which in the person of Jesus had already influenced the lives of the disciples. The only way in which they could understand themselves was as a group of messengers, who as disciples were meant to stand the test for all the others. In contrast to those other religious groups, the community, from the very beginning and until much later, called itself the community of God. This was how Israel had also understood itself. Therefore it could never regard itself as a separate community with a certain set of special religious observances to offer. It is probably for this reason, (and not only because of its difference from the Jewish synagogue), that it chose the word 'community', or more precisely, 'those called out by God', and not the more common word 'assembly' which meant 'synagogue'. This is also supported by certain other self-designations such as 'the saints', 'the elect', 'Israel', and 'the people of God'. The disciples of Jesus could not look upon themselves as a select, obedient *élite* around which the whole converted people of Israel would later gather, unlike some of the people of Qumran who did regard themselves in these terms. It is rather the case that their exclusiveness was something which could be described only in terms of their task; that is, those sent to the whole people of Israel. This is also why they did not allow themselves to be labelled as a Galilean sect which simply led its own quiet and peaceful life. Thus they, as it were, took over Jerusalem under the commission of their Lord so that they might claim the whole people of Israel for their God.

The disciples already knew of the reign which God had established in Jesus, and in the eschatological joy of their table-fellowship (during which they celebrated the Lord's Supper) they tasted its future glory. This led neither to reforms nor to revolutions. The formative and decisive moments which occurred in the course of the slow growth of this community towards something like a church, were clearly not determined by dogmatic formulations. Even the fact that they proclaimed Jesus as the Messiah was not sufficient to separate them from others. (They did this from very early on, because the title 'Christ', found everywhere in the New Testament, can only be explained on the grounds that the early Christians consciously took up and affirmed the mocking inscription above the cross, saying of those words: 'That is exactly what he is, King of the Jews'). A man like Rabbi Akiba, for example, living in the much more dogmatic age of a hundred years later, could be highly venerated as a teacher of Israel, even though he had hailed Bar Kochba as the Messiah and had thereby led the whole people into unspeakable misery. There were also the Enoch circles, groups which lived unopposed among the Jews even though they believed in the son of Man enthroned in heaven as Messiah. It was widely accepted that Enoch, Elijah and many others up to their own time had been saved from death and taken up into heaven by God, and called the sons and servants of God, because of their righteousness. But in the case of the growing community, what really distinguished them from others was their knowledge of God's action in Jesus. If the reign of God had really come upon them when Jesus called them to follow him, and when he called them once again into his service after his resurrection, even though they had failed him miserably, then obedience to the Law, the meticulous fulfilment of temple-observances, and even membership of the circumcised children of Abraham, could no longer be regarded as the most important things.

In fact, the actual separation of the community is something which is always bound up with their suffering. Those who did take these matters seriously expelled them. The group of Hellenists which had gathered around Stephen is driven out of Jerusalem, (Acts 7 and 8 : 1ff.), and, because of the persecution which had broken out against this group, its members engaged in a mission to the Samaritans and soon afterwards to the non-Jews in Syria. In A.D. 44, at a time when Agrippa's policy relied upon the support of the Pharisees, Peter was expelled, (Acts 12), while James, the brother of the Lord, who remained true to the Law, could still remain the leader of the community. Then, about A.D. 62, in spite of the exceptional faithfulness to the Law for which he was known, he himself was killed. Shortly after this the community fled from the endangered Jerusalem to Pella. It was always like this: Israel had to drive out the disciples because they realised that this community now regarded as absolute the newly-established reign of Jesus, not the Law, to which, nevertheless, the community outwardly conformed. This says nothing about whose guilt is the greater. Those who could not affirm that God had acted decisively in the cross and resurrection of Jesus, had no alternative but to admit that the disciples of Jesus took a different view from them with regard to that which was now the most important thing in their lives.

Many found themselves unable to go along with them. We therefore have to ask whether the life of the community can still be described in the same terms as the life led by those who followed Jesus. To this question we must answer Yes and No. No, because for one thing the crucifixion and resurrection of Jesus had taken place in the meantime. This posed the urgent question as to whether or not God in Jesus had himself really come into the world to bring salvation, to set men free and to call men to obedience. In the long run this was a question which could not be avoided, largely because of the denials of the disciples on Good Friday. From then on they could live only from the grace of Jesus' call to discipleship and from their having been called again after Easter, not from their own righteousness. All Israel, whose leaders had approved of this crucifixion and who at least to a certain extent shared some responsibility for it, were faced with these same strict alternatives. The same question had also to be faced by the Gentiles who in accepting the message of Jesus affirmed God's dealings with Israel, though they knew that they shared no part in it whatsoever, but knew also that they possessed no righteousness before God.

However, the answer is also Yes. Yes, to the extent that the life of the community is a life of boundless joy in the fact that God has once and for all established his reign of grace. Yes also, as long as this joy is not merely the acknowledgment of a particular state of affairs, but rather the joy of being

101

called to obedience by the power of God's Holy Spirit, and living from day to day by this grace. Yes, as long as this community does not seek to re-establish a new righteousness of its own, a righteousness based upon the 'correct' confession, or a righteousness of 'proper' Christian conduct. Even when such conduct may be said to consist in humility, or in an awareness of sin, or in suffering for its own sake which is incomprehensible to others, this would still be self-righteousness enough to separate the community from Israel and the world. And Yes also, as long as the obedience of the community is an obedience in freedom, in the sense that it is bound solely by the fact that day by day it receives the grace of its Lord Jesus Christ and so is called to service.

V

The difficulty which we face in our own time is perhaps that in normal circumstances we are not called upon to leave our homes or to give up our occupations in the way in which this is described in the Synoptic Gospels. Neither are we really dominated by other 'saviours', or doctrines of salvation to the extent that these endanger our lives; the situation which is described in the Johannine re-interpretation. Nor are we in danger of succumbing to the kind of enthusiasm which completely forgets the needs of our neighbour and which is concerned only with self-salvation; the kind of enthusiasm which Paul found in Corinth and elsewhere. This is why it is often very difficult for us really to understand all that has come to us in Jesus. This is why the righteousness of God which is established in Jesus Christ is so difficult for us to understand in any definite sense. It would be rather useless, if for strict moral reasons we should give up our homes or occupations in an effort to conform to the example of the first disciples, or for dogmatic reasons attempt to approach the Johannine ideal by putting all the emphasis on the pure saving grace of Christ, or even for religious reasons select and stress the mystery of baptism and its significance as a dying to all sin. If we were to do any of these things we would simply be putting ourselves in the centre of the picture. This would also mean cutting

102

ourselves off from those who can no longer understand what we now want to say. To do this would mean that the significance and importance of all that God has done in Jesus would become obscure rather than meaningful.

In order to find out what it means to be a disciple in our own day, we must perhaps return once again to Jesus' sayings about discipleship and to his actions. We must listen once again to the message of the Synoptics, and of Paul and John. This is not to say that we can find the pure truth about Jesus' words and actions only in the historical Jesus and not in the post-Easter witness. They come to us only through the post-Easter witness itself. Thus we have to return to these, because we have to learn and to understand anew the different post-Easter interpretations in the light of Jesus' Word and action.

When Jesus met Levi he met a man who was absorbed in his occupation, an occupation which separated him from God just in the same way as our occupations take up our time to such an extent that there is no room left for God, God's action and God's Word. When Jesus encountered Peter and Andrew, John and James, he met men who were in the midst of their daily task and who had very little time for God. Today our world is a world which is busily occupied, a world in which work is pursued with seriousness. Every achievement, including journeys to the Moon and to Venus, is considered important. Yet it seems that all this has very little to do with God. And this is because no one really knows any longer why these things are undertaken. Thus many endeavours are rendered quite meaningless, even to the extent that suicide is more often becoming the solution. Perhaps the church today should learn anew, in Jesus' words about discipleship and in his actions, that God has come into our life, that he wishes to give life a meaning and a task once again. And perhaps, in recognising the continuing activity of the risen Christ in the formation of the post-Easter community, it could learn that in Jesus, God has not merely come into the life of each individual to give it meaning, but that through fellowship and through the Christian community, he wishes to help the whole of society and give it a new meaning through the brotherhood of discipleship.

We must leave it there with these brief hints. Our theme

is by no means exhausted. To follow Jesus must always mean that we must trust him to lead us, that we do not attempt to take over the leadership ourselves. It also means that we must let him determine the way, and not prescribe for him, least of all prescribe theologically, the way which he wishes to take with us and our church into the future.

Notes to

DISCIPLESHIP AND CHURCH

1. In this connection see my essay: "Die 'Mystik' des Sterbens und Auferstehens mit Christus bei Paulus", in *Evangelische Theol.* 26, 1966. pp. 239ff.

2. Especially in his essay, "Gerechtigkeit Gottes", in *Z.Th.K.* 58, 1961, pp. 367-378.

3. I have tried to give an example of this in a short essay on the Healing of the Nobleman's Son, cf. *Evangelische Theol.* 1951, pp. 64-71.